SETTING THE PACE

FOR

BUSINESS SUCCESS

How To Maximize Your Potential and
Get What You Want

Danny Lanier

with

Marilyn Pincus

To: Joseph
wishing you all the best !
Danny Lanier 5/22/04

CORINTHIAN
BOOKS

Mt. Pleasant, S.C.

First edition. First printing, February 2002.

Publisher's Cataloging-in-Publication
(Provided by Quality Books. Inc.)

Lanier, Danny.
    Setting the pace for business success: how to maximize your potential and get what you want / Danny Lanier. — 1st ed.
    p. cm.
    Includes index.
    LCCN 2001096038
    ISBN 1-929175-30-2 (HC)
    ISBN 1-929175-49-3 (SC)

    1. Success in business.   I. Title

HF 5386.L36 2001   650.1
                        QBI01-201278

Corinthian Books
an imprint of The Côté Literary Group
P.O. Box 1898
Mt. Pleasant, S.C. 29465-1898
(843) 881-6080
www.corinthianbooks.com

Contents

ACKNOWLEDGMENTS

WRITING THIS BOOK has been a goal of mine for quite some time, and it has been extremely satisfying to make it a reality. So many people have helped to shape my life and my business experiences over the years. I am sure I will miss acknowledging someone; however, these are some of the individuals and groups that come to mind.

I thank my parents, the late Charles and Mabel Lanier, for bringing me into the world; my grandparents, the late Harvey and Katie Lanier, who raised me; and my high school teachers who had faith in me and saw my potential. My thanks also go to the late Bertha Tyler, my friend's mother, who helped me with my college expenses, and to my college professors, Dr. Jimmy King and Dr. Howard Carter, for their encouragement.

Many thanks to my wife, Rose, and my son, Danny, Jr., for supporting me during our many relocations and job changes. Their lives are different because they chose to support my efforts to succeed.

Acknowledgments also go to many of my coaches at AT&T and Lucent Technologies for helping to shape me and for challenging me to do my best. I also want to thank the thousands of colleagues who supported me in my various job assignments. You made me what I am today.

I thank my brothers, Harry, Sam, and Timmy, as well as my sister, Karen, for always being there for me.

Last, I acknowledge Marilyn Pincus for assisting me in writing this book. Marilyn, it has been a pleasure!

Danny Lanier
February 2002

THE CHOICE IS YOURS

During the mid-1980s, as I was making my way up the ladder at AT&T, people started asking me to share my "success secrets" with them. I was both surprised and flattered. I thought about my definition of success and the success methods I'd been using. I began to read all the books and articles I could find that were written by or about successful people. So while I moved my career forward and helped others do the same, I was also detailing a clear blueprint of what we were doing.

If you're hungry for this kind of know-how, this book is for you! The information contained in *Setting the Pace for Business Success: How to Maximize Your Potential and Get What You Want* will help you transform the circumstances you have into the circumstances you want.

Success means different things to different people. To some, success means money and power. To others, it means financial security and supportive relationships. It can also mean being the best in your profession. Booker T. Washington said, "Success is to be measured not so much by the position one holds in life as by the obstacles that were overcome while trying to succeed." His words inspired me throughout my career since overcoming obstacles has been a challenge for me since childhood. My definition of success focused primarily on being financially secure and able to retire at age 50. In the process, I wanted to build and maintain close relationships with my family and friends, travel around the globe, and help others realize their dreams.

It took me nearly half of my career to figure out that there are nine key steps to achieving success in business. While I had already enjoyed a fair amount of success, some of what I learned in the second half of my career would have been enormously valuable to me if I were exposed to it earlier. This is a key reason for writing this book. I want others to benefit from those insights early in their careers. What I learned is that the following nine principles are used by most successful business people. In the chapters that follow, you will become thoroughly familiar with all nine principles and how each one operates. Equally important are the assorted adventures peppered throughout the book, which vividly illustrate these success steps at work. In no time at all, you'll be saying, "If Danny can do it, I can do it, too!"

At A Glance

1. Accept Accountability For Your Life
2. Decide What You Want To Achieve
3. Develop Your Plan
4. Perform Like Your Career Depends On It
5. Surround Yourself With People Who "Make A Positive Difference"
6. Utilize "Exposure" For All It's Worth
7. Build A Reputation For Good Character
8. Keep A Positive Attitude
9. Learn To Deal With Adversity

SECTION ONE

1

ONE GOAL AT A TIME

AT AGE TWELVE, I set my first goal: get away from having to work in the fields under the hot sun. We're about to step back in time to visit my childhood years.

Earliest Memories

My parents split up, and somehow when I was about three years old, my two brothers and I ended up living with my grandparents, who owned and worked on their farm outside of Selma, Alabama. These are my earliest memories.

I started working in the fields when I was about six years old. To supplement family earnings, which were about $1,200 a year, my brothers and I also worked on neighboring farms gathering crops. I picked cotton, okra, and other vegetables from age six until about age seventeen.

We had to take afternoons off from school in order to work for the first six weeks of the school year. This meant we were behind in schoolwork by six weeks at the start of every school year.

To say that, in the years 1955-1967, an annual income of $1,200 for a family of five was at the low end of the poverty level is an understatement. Scratching out an existence was the priority. *School was what you did when there was no work to be done.*

Going to school without lunch money, or lunch, was fairly common for my brothers and me. Almost everybody had lunch they brought from home, or they could buy food at a nearby café. It was customary for classmates to sit together and eat and to say a prayer before the meal. Words of praise for the food we were about to receive were impossible to express under the circumstances, i.e., I didn't have food! I frequently hid behind a soda machine until lunchtime ended.

My grandparents' farm crops and the livestock (e.g., chickens, pigs, cows) supplied the ingredients for our evening meals. I suspect my grandparents didn't always have enough food to send us to school with lunch. I don't know. I do know they didn't have money to give us to buy lunch.

We didn't have television, a telephone, or a car, and most of those years we didn't own a radio. We didn't have a football, basketball, or baseball. We used a tin can as a ball, and a trash can with a missing bottom served as a target for making a goal. We played hopscotch and other games you could play that didn't require tools. We wore used clothes and most years we didn't wear shoes. There were no books in the house. I don't remember my grandparents ever helping us with schoolwork. That notion probably never entered their thoughts.

My grandfather believed a person has to make his own way in the world. *You have to do it. If something is to be, it's up to you to make it so.*

At age twelve, I set my first goal: get away from having to work in the fields under the hot sun. I set my goals in increments, one thing leading to the next. I would get a job where I didn't have to work under the sun or in a field. That meant finishing high school.

Grief And Loss

One night, my grandmother, who was seated directly across the table from me, suddenly screamed, reached for her head, stood up, and rushed to the bathroom. By the time I arrived to see what was wrong, she had collapsed. We picked her up, took her into the bedroom, and put her on the bed. We had absolutely no experience with such matters and spent some time trying to figure out what to do.

Our closest neighbor lived about one quarter of a mile away from us. We got the neighbor to drive us all to the hospital in Selma, about ten miles away. My brothers and I had no idea what was going on as we sat outside and waited. We noticed that adults around us were crying. We kept asking, "What's going on?" but nobody told us anything. Finally, we heard that she had suffered a heart attack. Just a few hours earlier, she had been working in the fields with us, as usual. She died and we went into shock. Life without our grandmother was unthinkable.

Our mother came to her parents' home to attend the funeral and she stayed. This was in May 1966. I was a junior in high school.

In April 1967, less than one year after my grandmother's death, we experienced another shock. My mother said she wouldn't fix breakfast one morning because she didn't feel well. By late afternoon, my mother had been hospitalized. We were summoned from school to the hospital and jolted by the news that our 39-year-old mother was dead. I leave it to you to imagine what the impact of these two losses was on my brothers and me.

Family Decisions

Relatives arrived and questions had to be answered. What are we going to do about the farm? What are we going to do about this? What are we going to do about that?

I was less than two months away from my high school

graduation at the time, and they decided to sell half the farm. By graduation day, the land had been sold, and after bills were paid, a small sum of money remained. It was sufficient to purchase airline tickets for my brothers and me. And so it came to pass that we flew to Albany, New York, to spend the summer with my mother's sister.

Hello To Opportunity

My teachers had encouraged me to fill out college applications and although I didn't have money at the time, I went through the process. I was accepted at Tuskegee. I sent in a $100 deposit and decided to attend the school long enough to use up my money! But a friend of mine was also accepted at Tuskegee, and his mother told me that if I would go to college with her son, she would help me take care of my financial needs. The plan was for me to work during summers and whenever I could, and my friend's mother would fill in the money gaps. (By the way, there were sixty-two students in our high school graduating class and only two of us attended college. I suspect this generous woman wanted us both to earn college degrees. We did.)

I talked to the college financial aid officer and the upshot was that I received a government grant to pay my tuition. I worked cleaning bathrooms and doing other chores to earn money for room and board.

Time To Tell

I have never told this story, in so much detail, to anyone. First, it's painful to recall the impoverishment and loss but, more important, I don't think anybody wants to hear this stuff. Successful people tend to accentuate the positive. When my colleagues talk about television shows they remember from 1955 to 1965 and I say, "We never had television," they think I'm kidding. Information, experiences, and stimuli that most Americans were exposed to in those years are enigmas to me. When I think back to ages 5 to 15, it's like peering into a dark hole. It served no useful purpose to dwell on these facts and I didn't.

As time went by, however, my beginning became more and more relevant in terms of the transition from there to where I went from there. It became important for me to let people know that if I did it — almost anyone can do it!

When I interviewed for my very first job, after graduation, I was asked a question that had something to do with adversity. It was the first time I revealed some of my early history.

I told the interviewer that when I was in the first grade, the teachers seated us at different tables depending upon our abilities. There were the A, B, and C tables. I was at the B table, or the almost B table, as I recollect.

My friend, Richard, was seated at the A table. I asked Richard for a piece of paper. A girl seated near to Richard said, "Don't give him paper. He can't write."

She believed something as small as one piece of paper would be wasted if Richard gave it to me. I never forgot that.

By the time I was in seventh grade, and probably earlier than that, I was the number one student in my grade level and that continued through the first semester in my senior year.

I graduated from high school as the number two student. I got a B in chemistry and my friend, Marvin, got an A.

Questions Without Answers

Where was my mother when we were young? What caused my parents to split up, and where was my father? Why did these people virtually disappear from our lives for such a long period of time?

I know that in those years many young black adults moved north in search of jobs. They earned very little and managed only to sustain themselves. Otherwise, what I know is merely conjecture and wouldn't be of value to you. But here's something that contributes to my peace of mind today and so I share it with you.

My father lived in Detroit and didn't communicate with us when we were growing up, but eventually, he moved back to Alabama. By then, I had graduated from college and was living with my wife, Rose, and son, Danny, Jr., in Dallas. We returned to Selma often to visit and I started to see my father. He was proud of me and enjoyed telling people that I was his son. I don't know why this was so but I suspect it was because I was beginning to enjoy a little business success at the time. I allowed him, if you will, his tendency to boast.

And so when he passed away, I was happy that I had made peace with him, didn't hold any grudges, and treated him with respect.

I'm thankful, too, that my mother lived with us during the final period of her short life because it gave me the chance to know her and learn that she was a person who had a "good heart."

Motivational Gems

We can sit back in our easy chairs and pontificate about how it is that some people move through adversity while others are crushed by it. I will only tell you what I know about myself. I didn't want to pick cotton or work in the fields. So part of my motivation came from getting away from something. But another part was believing in possibilities and trusting that if you are trying to help yourself, other people are more likely to help you. There has been evidence of that throughout my life and my career.

Believing in positive outcomes and believing that if you are trying to help yourself, other people are more likely to help you are powerful phenomena. A seventh grade teacher was probably the first person to confirm this truth, although at the time, I didn't recognize it. I wanted to play in the school band and couldn't afford the instrument. This teacher purchased it for me. A few years later, when my brother Harry and I wanted to play on the basketball team, we had to stay after classes to practice and missed the bus ride home. One of the teachers drove us to stay overnight with a friend who lived in town. That teacher picked us up the next morning and drove us to school.

A couple of high school teachers encouraged us to attend college. Even though I said, "Yes I would like to go to college," I didn't see any possible way that I could afford it. But I already told you about that.

My one-goal-at-a-time sequence matured. Get out of the fields. Finish high school. Finish college. Get a job with a large company. And all the while, the Beatles contention that "I'll get by with a little help from my friends" was especially meaningful to me. I am where I am today because of a little help from my friends.

You Can Get Here From There — I Did

Prior to my retirement, I held a number of key positions with Lucent Technologies and AT&T, including Accounting Manager, Factory Controller, Business Unit Controller, and Financial Vice President. At the time of my retirement, I was Global Financial Process Director for Lucent Technologies, a company generating over $30 billion in revenues annually. I was responsible for the six major financial centers that processed most of Lucent's customer billing, payroll, accounts payable, and accounts receivable.

Lucent had financial functions spread all over the globe. My responsibilities took me to Singapore, China, the Caribbean Islands, and Latin America, which includes Central and South America. On more than one occasion, I traveled to Mexico, Panama, Brazil, Argentina, and Costa Rica to conduct business, and that's only part of the story. Illustrations of career adventures, challenges, and triumphs are scattered throughout this book.

My career was more challenging and financially rewarding than that little boy living outside of Selma, Alabama, could have imagined in his most fantastic dreams.

On The Drawing Board

If you think about your life plan as being the master plan and your career plan as a subplan, or a portion of the overall plan, you'll recognize that you're the master planner. You'll adjust plans from time to time because you don't control all the variables. Still, while you're seated at that drawing board, you're in an enviable position. My plan included the following:

(1) Pay for our son's education

(2) Retire at age 50

(3) Be debt free

(4) Become a millionaire

(5) Retire healthy and happy

(6) Rejoice with Rose. (We're married 30 years as I write this book.)

Each goal has been realized. I know I'm a lucky man! And you know I've got the credentials to help take you where you want to go.

This brings me to one more aspect of my master plan. Success to me involves not only achieving but also giving back — helping others. I have a strong desire to transform the world into a better place within the space of time allotted to me by utilizing the opportunities and access available to me.

2

THE PERFECT CANDIDATE

T HIS BOOK IS WRITTEN for people who have at least five years of work experience. As I mentioned earlier, I set my goals in increments, one thing leading to the next.

I would get a job where I didn't have to work under the sun or in a field. That meant finishing high school.

Once you've reached a particular goal, you set a new one and then you reach it and you set a new one. From each level, you're able to see new opportunities.

If you're ready to *maximize your potential and get what you want,* you have already seen, felt, heard, and tackled some of the stuff that comes early on in the workplace. In short, you have a frame of reference and can relate to the issues.

On the other hand, if you don't have five years of work experience but care to come along as we map the journey, by all means, you're welcome to join us!

Prerequisites

Although I spent my career working for large companies, people working in small companies and entrepreneurs who operate their own businesses are perfect candidates for

Setting the Pace for Business Success. That's because steps, methods, strategies, and practices that lead to the desired results are universal and apply in all business environments.

I'm a college graduate and have a master's degree, but you're a perfect candidate for *Setting the Pace for Business Success* without this kind of educational background. Formal education is always recommended and is always an asset. Graduate school degrees, however, are not, in the long term, what make the difference between those who succeed and those who don't.

Finally, your gender, race, age, religious background, state of health, country of birth, and anything else that helps to describe you are factors to reckon with in the broad scheme of things. All come into play in every working person's life, and you may experience some discrimination. These, however, aren't overriding issues when it comes to setting lofty goals and attaining them. If, for whatever reason, you believe you're not able to set the pace for business success the same as anyone else, you can shed that perception.

To sum up, the perfect candidate for *Setting the Pace for Business Success* has:

- Five years of work experience
- No need for work experience in a big company setting
- No need for exceptional educational achievements
- An ability to shed perceptions that suggest he or she doesn't measure up
- The desire for a better life
- A willingness to try new things

The perfect candidate is ready to accept that success is possible and that he or she can achieve it!

Passion

It's almost impossible to utter the word "passion" without giving it emphasis! When we talk of passion, we speak of strong desire. Our emotions are engaged and dance onto center stage. What do you want out of life? What excites you? Are you animated when you respond to these two questions? If so, you're probably passionate about attaining your goals. If not, you may want to plug in goals that get your adrenaline pumping because one of the attributes common to all those who seek and attain success is passion. Sometimes your passion needs protection from people who say such things as:

"You're not being practical."

"I think you should become a physician like your father."

"People from our race never make it big in the banking industry."

Almost everyone has been exposed to this kind of comment. If you set aside plans that once inspired you and started down other roads, you may want to think about where you're heading. When headed in the right direction, you're content. Being content as you go may be why you get there! At the moment, however, we're not examining the dynamics of how passion for attaining goals operates. We're acknowledging that it does operate!

Just For Emphasis

People in many arenas accomplish seemingly impossible feats based upon strong desires. The sports world immediately comes to mind. Another area that may be less obvious is overcoming medical challenges. In the book *The Pain Cure* by Dharma Singh Khalsa, M.D. with Cameron Stauth (Warner Books, 1999), the doctor observes:

> The more information you have about chronic pain, the less likely you will be to engage in faulty thinking about it. . . . It's also important that you dispel any cynicism you may have about the mind-power effect. Don't think of it as a means of fooling yourself, but as a force that literally puts mind over

matter . . . Don't tell yourself something you don't really believe. It won't work because you're too smart to believe your own lies.

The doctor provides compelling arguments complete with statistics that underscore how a powerful desire to achieve something is the prelude to achieving it.

You supply the passion; *Setting the Pace for Business Success* will spotlight the tools you can use to get what you want.

To Sum Up:
1. Faulty thinking works to defeat a person. This means if you're working to achieve a goal that someone else has set for you, unless you have made that goal your own, you labor at a disadvantage.
2. Believing in what you want to attain is an essential step in maximizing your potential to get what you want.

A Question of Passion!

The following quiz is only meant to provoke some this-way, that-way kind of thinking. In other words, answer the questions as best you can and shake up your little gray cells!

If you agree with the next statements, circle the 10 rating.

If you partially agree, circle the 5 rating.

If you disagree, circle zero.

(1) There's no question that I have a passion for chocolate, fine wine, driving new cars, taking vacations in exotic places, or for something that I indulge in from time to time. Accordingly, I know what passion feels like!

10   5   0

(2) Although I think of some items as luxury items (e.g.,

tickets to the opera, custom-made silk shirts), I refuse to forego them completely. Accordingly, I indulge in some of my passions!

10   5   0

(3) If I close my eyes and envision being immersed in activities that please me (e.g., playing tennis, getting a massage, listening to fine music, piloting my own airplane, strolling in an art gallery) I enjoy the exercise!

10   5   0

(4) The reason I purchased *Setting the Pace for Business Success* is that I'm convinced I can get what I want and am looking for better ways to proceed.

10   5   0

Score: A score of 40 suggests that you're a passionate person and know it! A score of 20 suggests that you're not pulling your own strings. Ouch, it hurts to have someone else pull your strings! A score of 0 suggests you didn't take this quiz seriously! Either that or you have buried your passions deep and out of reach. You wouldn't be the first person to do this, but you will want to disassociate from this group so that you're in a stronger position to maximize your potential and get what you want!

Broaden Your Perspective

By now, you're probably convinced of the value of being passionate about your career goal. Sometimes it's useful to step away from people who don't support you in order to achieve what it is that makes you passionate. Other times you simply can't see the forest for the trees.

Step back and the entire forest may come into focus. Do what's necessary to convince yourself that the target you're shooting for is the target you want to hit or it is not.

Labels That Mislead

Just like the A B C tables the teacher set up in my first grade classroom, with the A table reserved for only the best students, other labels creep up in life. For many of us, being told we aren't among the best, especially at a young age, is hurtful. Worse than feeling hurt is accepting that this label is accurate.

It's also damaging to pin on your own negative label. At one time in my life, I labeled myself Not-the-Master-of-Ceremonies type. *I can't speak in front of a group!*

Since that time, I've spoken in front of many groups. Some audiences numbered more than a thousand, and on numerous occasions, translators had to translate my words into several languages because I communicated with people from many different countries.

If I permitted my Not-the-Master-of-Ceremonies-type label to remain firmly ingrained, I would have cheated myself! That label did nothing to help me.

Limit Or Liberate

I know I'm not a detail person. But if I've got to deal with all the details in order to complete a job, I'll be a detail person.

It was limiting to label myself, Not-the-Master-of-Ceremonies type. It's liberating to know that I'm not a detail person. I delegate the details to people who like to work on them. BUT I know I can be a detail person when it's necessary.

Attributes That Are Common To All Achievers

Successful people tend to behave in recognizable ways. I've traveled most of the globe and read extensively about other cultures. I'm still looking for that strange individual who doesn't have any of the common characteristics that successful people have and has managed to attain success. I don't think I'll ever locate such a person.

You already know that passion is one of these attributes. In the chapters that follow, I'll lay out the others. Before I do, however, here's something else to consider.

Boost Your Chances

Your chances for success increase dramatically if you go with your strengths. After you identify your passion, ask yourself if it matches or makes the best use of your strengths. You'll do some self-analysis to determine if your chosen goal puts you on the fast lane for success. After all, your ultimate goal is to attain success.

Let's say someone named Sara is 27 years old and has a strong desire to be a concert pianist, even though she can't play the piano. If Sara has to earn her living now, you wouldn't bet on Sara doing it as a concert pianist. If Sara is a terrific salesperson and enjoys managing others, she may wish to align with the field of music in some other capacity.

Would Sara excel at managing concert pianists' careers? Perhaps. It comes closer to partnering her passion with her strengths.

Recognizing Strengths

Partnering your goals with your strengths takes self-analysis and objectivity. That's not an easy combination to employ since most people find it difficult to be objective about themselves. As a matter of fact, someone may suggest that you follow Plan X instead of Plan Y because he doesn't believe you have an aptitude to be successful with Plan Y. That individual is probably being objective, even though you may interpret what he says as negative.

Individuals tend to be subjective, and subjectivity almost by definition comes complete with blind spots. You may not see how good you are at some things. Or you may believe you're good but you're on shaky ground until someone reinforces your suspicions. Then, too, you may completely dismiss talents and abilities believing — anybody can do that!

Striking A Balance

I think seeking input is very important and suggest that you listen carefully to what others tell you about your career choice. Be ready to dismiss comments from the naysayers who would have you abandon your strong desires but, at the same time, be ready to accept observations that may help you better understand your strengths.

People observe things that you do well and things you don't do well. But they won't always tell you, especially if it's something that you don't do well. Most people don't want to hurt your feelings.

Position Your Goals With Your Strengths

Illustration: Nelson Murphy, Chief Financial Officer, Telegis Networks, Inc., Los Gatos, California, worked for AT&T when we first met. In a letter dated October 10, 2000, he wrote, "Danny served as a support manager, a coach and a mentor to me throughout the last fifteen years of my career. . . . In the last nine years, Danny and I have not worked directly together; however, I have continued to seek out and solicit his advice and counsel on key decisions for me. . . . He [Danny] has recommended for me several roles that on the surface seemed "off the beaten path" but that in hindsight were directly to the heart of the developmental objective

. . . . His creativity has helped me follow a career path that was not inherently obvious at the time but in hindsight very thorough, ordered and effective."

3

MODUS OPERANDI

Do you remember the first promise you made to yourself? Did you keep it?

Some folks amble along and take whatever comes to them. These people have only to react, and frequently they're pleased with results. They probably set early goals: finish high school, get a job, marry, have a family, live happily ever after. Most people have some plans because they're expected to do so by family, teachers, friends, and society. Look at the first few advertisements you see today and you'll see suggestive selling out in the open.

"Join the Navy and see the world."

"Use Brand X toothpaste and Brand Y deodorant and members of the opposite sex won't be able to resist your charms."

"Learn how to drive 18-wheel trucks cross-country; make good money; be your own boss."

Other sales pitches aren't so easy to identify. Some of us feel pressured or guilty by virtue of other people's expectations for us and believe we have no choice but to fall in step. It's less hassle to move along putting one step in front of the other and to do what's suggested or expected. **Virtually all successful people operate differently.** They survey the horizon and take charge. They pick a destination and map the journey. Of course, they're subject to outside influences but they're proactive.

Let's say someone named Jake at age 17 knew he was willing to work hard, and he wanted to earn an excellent living. He excelled in college science courses and started to think about becoming a physician. At about that time, two of his friends left college to start a restaurant. The restaurant idea came to them after Jake and his friends successfully operated a late-night snack business on campus. It was a tempting prospect but Jake didn't join them. He finished college, went to medical school, and before long, had a thriving private practice. He enjoyed his work and made an excellent living. So did his two buddies. They never finished college but they owned and operated a successful restaurant chain. Each person initiated opportunities. Each was proactive.

You're Not Alone

A seventh grade teacher purchased a musical instrument for me. Another teacher provided transportation so that I could play on the basketball team. These are early memories of receiving "a little help from my friends."

You may want to take a moment to identify your own personal network of friends. It's comforting to know you don't have to do everything alone. This knowledge makes the journey to attain your goals a little less formidable.

You're Reading This Book, Aren't You?

I wrote it for you and recommend that you use it as a reference book after you finish reading it. Send e-mail to me right now via my website if you care to do so. I'll respond. Now that's support! You're not alone.

(My web address: www.maxpocoach.com.)

By the way, when I graduated from college I didn't have a single relative present but I was proud of me for me. There are times when you're not alone because essentially *you're with yourself.* It's a concept worth noting.

My Turn

You're reading my current goal achievement. Why now? Why write this book when I'm no longer on the playing field? One of the reasons is perspective. How sweet it is to look back and see it all so clearly from this vantage point. And how rewarding it is to lay it out for you to use. Remember, too, I learned some key strategies late in my career but I'm making them available to you early in your career. Some of the things I write about I didn't use, and with some, it was simply too late to get the full benefit of the strategies. It's my hope that you'll make use of these insights now.

Oh, there's more. I'm moving on. Shortly after retiring, I founded MaxpoCoach, a company specializing in executive coaching and personal leadership development programs. I believe that *Setting the Pace for Business Success: How to Maximize Your Potential and Get What You Want* compliments these programs.

It may interest you to know that just as I recommend that you do something you feel passionate about, I feel passionate about operating MaxpoCoach. I've been involved in executive coaching and personal leadership development for a long time. At Lucent, I was an advisor to the Alliance of Black Lucent Employees and a mentor for participants in Lucent's Financial Leadership Development Program. I'm no stranger to executive coaching and personal leadership development. I continue to receive notes and calls that report on achievements almost weekly. These come from co-workers and others who sought my counsel, and whenever I receive them, they serve to make my day! Let me give you just one example and you'll see what I mean:

In November 2000, Sandy D. Welfare, Accounts Payable/ Treasury, Global Financial Service, Lucent Technologies, Australia and New Zealand, e-mailed the following: "My manager came all the way to Sydney to give me my year-end appraisal. She stated that I was a 'fantastic and dynamic leader' who had the ability to 'both support my team members, and inspire them to do greater things.' She also stated that I had an incredible ability to deal with difficult people and situations . . . ."

Modus Operandi (MO) Under Construction

Be aware that virtually everyone's MO is first influenced by "taking what comes to you," such as accepting help from a grade school teacher. But, once you move into the driver's seat and design and/or follow the map you drew to reach your destination, your MO undergoes change. You may want to have your MO appraised while it's in this under-construction stage. The process is similar to being watched by a ballet master. He quickly notices steps that should be perfected. He shouts instructions to dance students, and potential bad habits are eliminated before they form. (See Section Two, "A Topnotch Coach: How To Find One — How To Be One," for details.)

4

ON STAGE, BUT IN THE SHADOWS

Courage isn't widely discussed in management books, yet it plays a key role in achieving business success. Later, when you've reached your goals, others who discouraged you will inevitably ask, "How did you do that?"

In a moment, you'll grasp how this phenomenon works, and you'll be steady as you go!

Let's begin with quotations from some well-known people. You'll notice they don't always use the word "courage," but I think you'll agree that courage or lack of it is at the heart of the matter.

• "The people who get on in this world are the people who get up and look for the circumstances they want, and, if they can't find them make them." (George Bernard Shaw)

• "Even a fool knows you can't touch the stars, but it doesn't stop a wise man from trying." (Harry Anderson)

• "One can never consent to creep, when one feels an impulse to soar." (Helen Keller)

• "Whatever you can do, or dream you can, begin it. Boldness has genius, power, and magic in it." (Goethe)

- "Courage is doing what you're afraid to do. There can be no courage unless you're scared." (Eddie Rickenbacker)

- "Success is to be measured not so much by the position one holds in life as by the obstacles that were overcome while trying to succeed." (Booker T. Washington)

- "Courage is resistance to fear, mastery of fear — not absence of fear." (Mark Twain)

- "I have great respect for any (person) who makes (his/her) own way in life." (Winston Churchill)

- "History's greatest achievers have always managed themselves." (Peter Drucker)

- "Everything comes to him who hustles while he waits." (Thomas Edison)

- "Successful people do the things that others don't like to do." (E. M. Gray)

- "Only those who risk going too far can possibly find out how far one can go." (T. S. Elliot)

- "Our greatest glory is not in never failing but in rising each time we fail." (Confucius)

- "It is fatal to enter any war without the will to win it." (General Douglas MacArthur)

- "The difference between the impossible and the possible lies in a person's determination." (Tommy Lasorda)

- "If you want to manifest your desires you must be accountable for everything in your life." (Debbie Ford)

- "Don't let anyone discourage you or shake your confidence." (Danny Lanier)

By the way, if quoting other people serves to broaden your perspective and helps buoy your courage, be alert to inspiring observations that proliferate in books, articles, and sermons. Jot down favorites and refer to them often. I tracked many of the quotations listed above on the Internet using the search engine Google.com and the keywords "Famous-People and Quotations."

Discouragement Phenomenon

I specified that if you grasp why it is that some people discourage you, you'd be able to remain steady as you go. Mark Twain said it well: **"Keep away from people who try to belittle your ambitions. Small people always do that, but the really great make you feel that you, too, can become great."**

Abraham Lincoln expressed it this way, "Always bear in mind that your own resolution to succeed is more important than any other one thing." And I, Danny Lanier, agree that people who discourage you are small minded. This may be because they're frightened or jealous or not well informed or a mixture of all these and more. Why they are small minded isn't important. What is important is that you're not small minded! And if you counter messages of discouragement with Mr. Lincoln's words of wisdom that your own resolution to succeed is more important than any other one thing, you'll be working with a winning strategy.

STEP 1:
Accept Accountability For Your Life

So many people allow the expectations of others to guide them through life and never look within themselves for answers to who they are and what they can become. We're influenced by our parents, friends, teachers, and colleagues, but at the end of the day, it is you who must decide what you are about and what you want to become.

Recognize that unless you accept accountability for your life, your career, and your finances, a lot of time is wasted, and blame is dished out in large portions with nothing productive to show for it.

I once said, "It's your fault," to an associate who won a company contest. "Sure," he replied, sounding as though he had nothing to do with it and that it was all up to Lady Luck. The fact is, he entered the contest. He made 98 sales calls, which turned out to be more calls than anyone else in his division made in that contest month. These actions were within his control. Winning was his fault — blame the win on him!

Every day you make decisions on matters of every kind.

- Should I buy a house or rent an apartment?
- Should I work late or leave early to attend my son's baseball game?
- Should I give Tom credit for finding the mistake or not mention him?

If you decide to. . .

- Buy a house, and housing prices increase in your neighborhood by 10 percent in the first year, you can take a bow. "I was smart to buy this house. If I waited a year to buy, I probably couldn't have afforded this house!" It's not likely that you're responsible for the 10 percent rise in value for homes in the neighborhood but you are responsible for making a decision to buy a house. You had options.
- Attend your son's baseball game. If he hits his first home run, you're there to experience the joy. He is enormously proud and happy to have you with him. "I'll remember this day forever, Dad." You didn't gaze into a crystal ball and know ahead of time that your eight-year-old was going to hit a home run, but you knew he wanted you to be at the game and you made that a priority.
- Mention Tom in your report and he receives accolades from top management, but they also quietly take note of your character trait — giving credit where credit is

due. You could have left Tom out and even alluded to having played the major role in locating the mistakes. After all, you penned the report.

The Devil Made Me Do It

Successful people are accountable and not willing or able to put the blame on other people or circumstances beyond their control. They don't accept circumstances beyond their control as a viable excuse. Do you? (Of course, you can't arrange for sunny weather on the day of the picnic but you might postpone the picnic and treat everyone to a day at the bowling alley.)

Get Over It!

As author and trainer Debbie Ford said, "If you want to manifest your desires, you must be accountable for everything in your life."

I could have agreed that . . .

- My family is so poor that I can't go to college. (I did go to college.)
- My spouse wants to live in Georgia and is upset about selling our beautiful home, leaving her job, and moving far away from friends and family. I'll turn down a job offer to advance in the company because it means moving to New Jersey. (We talked about this move as necessary and agreed we would eventually move back to Georgia. I accepted the job offer and we moved.)
- The money they're offering me is so much more a month than I'm earning. It makes sense to opt for the money even though I'll detour from my career path. (I didn't accept the job.)

And so it goes. . . . There are always reasons why you shouldn't, couldn't, didn't do something. Get over it! Focus on the reasons why you should, can, and shall and get on with it. When you make mistakes, and you will, just keep moving forward.

Illustration: This true story comes under the heading: DUMB! In the first year of my career at AT&T, I was sent to attend an out-of-state training session. When I arrived at the airport with two co-workers, we learned there was a long delay between our arrival and the time that a bus was going to be available to take us to the training center. Sid and I decided we would use the time to have a few drinks. Jimmy was going to wait for the bus. He ultimately missed the first bus because he was trying to locate us. By the time the second bus arrived and we weren't there, he took it. So we missed the second bus, and since we had several hours to wait for the next bus, we decided to continue doing what we had been doing.

When Sid and I finally got on a bus to take us to the training center, there was a manager on the bus who was friendly with our boss. This manager told our boss what he had observed. As a result, our boss called us in to his office when we returned. He took the time and trouble to coach us but he also grounded us. We weren't allowed to travel to attend company functions for almost one year.

It's Not Too Late

If you don't have a history of being accountable for everything in your life, start today! Recognize that being accountable counts!   Use this information to better control your destiny. By the way, accountability is inextricably interwoven with character. (If character were a cake, accountability would be an indispensable ingredient.) Good character is recognized as an attribute that is shared by successful people. The broad topic of character is discussed at length in the next chapter.

STEP 2:
Decide What You Want To Achieve

By looking within and identifying your strengths, you'll be able to narrow the list of possible options and decide on a vision for your life. Your vision will serve as a guide for your plans and actions as you transform yourself to become what you desire. You'll set goals along the way to guide you and measure your progress.

What do you want out of life? What excites you?

Do these questions sound familiar? They were introduced earlier when the topic of passion was explored. More needs to be said! Since you're not a newcomer to the business world, you may believe this is a curious time to ask/answer these questions. It's not.

Your chances for success increase exponentially if you make choices that mesh with your strengths. Until these questions are answered, detour signs may keep popping up on your journey to success. The problem with that is you may never reach your destination.

Below you'll find 20 questions I prepared to assist you to do a little self-examination. Be aware, however, some well-known career assessment inventories have been devised by experts. Myers-Briggs is a popular one. A trained career consultant or career counselor may administer and help interpret these inventories. Your aptitudes, values, interests, skills, personality, strengths, areas of development, learning style, and more are open to scrutiny.

You may determine that this is something you want to do. If so, do obtain the services of an expert. Costs for an assessment administered via your computer and followed up with a telephone consultation may be upwards of $60 (see: www.careers-by-design.com). By the way, I offer you this information as a result of my perusing the Web. Please don't mistake it for an endorsement or recommendation, and do remember, I'm not an assessment expert.

Would The Real Strengths Step Forward, Please!

Don't ponder the questions. Supply short, top-of-the-head answers. If you can't supply an answer quickly, skip the question and move onto the next question. Before you begin, list the numbers 1 - 20 on a piece of paper. Write your answer next to the number that matches the number of the question. Answers should reflect your workplace behavior.

1. What do I do well at work?
2. Would my co-workers agree?
3. Which characteristics or experiences make me unique?
4. What was my proudest accomplishment within the last 12 months?
5. Do I always want to be the lead person?
6. Which phrase best describes me: detail person or big-picture person?
7. What is my least favorite job task?
8. Do I ask for help when I need it?
9. Am I a confident negotiator?
10. Do I like most people?
11. Do I prefer to work alone?
12. Am I a good communicator?
13. Do I listen carefully?
14. Do I learn how to operate new office equipment easily?
15. Am I patient?
16. Which one word best describes how I relate to criticism? Anger. Interest. Ignore.
17. Can I be a success if I don't earn a lot of money?
18. Am I willing to earn continuing education credits?
19. Do I meet deadlines?
20. Can I handle multiple tasks without having a meltdown?

Interpretation

Write two headings on your paper: Easy Pace and High Energy. Examine the answers you jotted next to numbers 1 - 20 and place as many as possible under one of the headings. If you wrote "meet deadlines" and believe you do because you're enthusiastic, well organized, and have lots of energy, jot the words "meet deadlines" under High Energy. Is the list of responses under Easy Pace long? If so, it suggests you don't want to work in an environment where there are ever-changing demands and lots of activity. You can repeat the assessment with any two headings you choose: Team Player or Solo Operator; High-tech or High-touch. In other words, you can design your own categories to assess your strengths.

The essence of this Q & A is to let you know that strengths can be measured. If you've never taken the time to think about whether or not you're a good listener or communicator, you're forced to think about it. I believe that reflection is important. It takes a sharp eye and some imagination to place your answers under headings that make sense, but it is one way to better understand yourself and your strengths.

Add BOTF To The Mix

Another reason to attempt personal assessment is to recognize that you may not be very good at it! In fact, you may need help. With that said, I offer you a powerful tool — Being Open to Feedback (BOTF). It's not at all mysterious, and it certainly is an old-fashioned tried-and-true aid. You can easily arrange to make the most of it, and you may already recognize the value of BOTF! BOTF virtually eliminates your blind spots. BOTF may reveal that you're better than you think you are.

This is a powerful tool you won't want to ignore as you strive to assess your strengths. Frequently, managers and co-workers supply feedback. You've got to be alert to this kind of incoming information. Use the best of it and discard the rest of it. It's easier to accept what mentors and coaches have to tell you since they're typically seasoned at supplying feedback and don't do it indiscriminately. As a matter of fact, you'll probably want to seek a coach or mentor and ask for his or her involvement and let that individual know that you're BOTF!

Now That You Know

"Vision is the art of seeing things invisible." So wrote the eighteenth-century English author Jonathan Swift. His remark is still veracious. I say, practice the art! Here's how: See it. Say it. Write it. If these instructions sound familiar, you probably first heard them when you were a young student memorizing lists of spelling words. The same approach works now.

See Where You're Going

Do you see yourself working from a desk in the administrative executive office? Will you have a leadership position in the research and development department? Maybe you're focused on international sales and playing a key role in the company's expansion plans. Fix the goal in your mind. See it!

Talk About Your Dreams

Say it to your spouse or family members and friends. Mention your dreams to people who can make it happen or help you make it happen.

Write It

Write it in your daily diary or someplace where you'll see it often. One successful restaurateur I know keeps a note in his money clip. The current one has four words: "Award-winning wine cellar." This guy is a master achiever. Since this vision has his full attention, prestigious awards for the wine collection are practically guaranteed.

When you see it, say it, write it, a curious thing happens. Your vision is no longer invisible. Look out, World, dreams are in the process of being realized! Now, you're ready to roll up your sleeves and conceptualize the kind of sacrifice that may be necessary to reach your goals.

Illustration: At one point in my career, I knew that another New Jersey tour would be necessary, and I discussed it with my family. New Jersey would never be our home of choice because we wanted to live in Georgia, so it would be a sacrifice for the family to relocate. At the same time, the company headquarters was housed in New Jersey. So when the opportunity presented itself, we were ready. We knew it was necessary to position me for the next level of career growth.

I used to say that the cost of living in New Jersey was high. I used to say it was the snow. Later, I came to realize it's the absence of convenience. Near our home in Georgia, for example, you can go to a different restaurant every night and never drive more than 30 minutes from home. You can do it for an entire month and not return to the same restaurant twice.

Many Times The Good Doesn't Come Easy

Some of the sacrifices you and your loved ones make to achieve your business goals are serious business. Absence of convenience is a frivolous concern compared to when you have a son in his last year of high school and relocation for him at that time would be 100 percent disruptive.

In fact, it happened to us and we three made a heart-wrenching decision. Our son, Danny, stayed with friends in Dallas so that he could complete his last year of school. At the time, Rose and I had a relatively new Georgia address. It was hard on all of us and especially difficult for Rose.

If you and those you love aren't willing or able to make the sacrifices that go with your vision, S-T-O-P. All may not be lost if you approach obstacles in a creative manner and if all parties are comfortable with the reasons why and the decisions made. Admittedly, that's a tall order. It's also necessary if you're determined to make your vision visible!

Negotiation
When I was in graduate school working on my MBA, there was a computer class that was in conflict with my work schedule. I wrote some computer programs six or eight years earlier and actually wrote some very significant programs at one of my previous jobs. I spoke with the school department head and asked if I were able to get a letter from my previous boss outlining what I had accomplished, could I have this class waived? He agreed. I made the request and received a nice letter outlining specifically what I had done. The class was waived.

Negotiation is a valuable tool to use to side-step obstacles. In fact, sharp negotiation skills may be needed to help translate your vision into reality.

Be aware:
- The more you use negotiation techniques, the better you become at negotiating.
- Create a blank page in your mind. Use your ears and your eyes. Listen carefully and take note of body language, if possible, so that you quickly understand what's important to the other person. If you're not listening, if you're competing with the other guy to talk, if what's on your mind is filling your thoughts, you're going to blow it. You need to know what's on the other person's mind so that you can begin to develop a plan. Use your creativity to arrive at a mutually agreeable decision. Until you know what *bugs* the other person, you're nowhere.

The fact is, we negotiate all the time. I remember one afternoon my wife called me out of the blue from her office and suggested that we go to OfficeMax at 6:00 P.M. She knew I needed some office supplies for my home office. Now, OfficeMax happens to be near the mall and my wife loves to shop. Since I'm home all day, when I need office supplies, I could probably go to the store at 2:00 P.M. and avoid traffic but I appreciated the offer. I asked Rose, "Am I running the risk of having to stop at the mall if we go to OfficeMax together?" Of course, I already knew the answer. This brings us to another key negotiation point:

- Listen for what's said and what's not said! One of the greatest negotiation skills is the ability to risk and to observe. The real turning point in negotiation is when you know exactly what the other person's priority is. If you reach that point, that's when you prepare to cut the deal of a lifetime.
- Ask a probing question. Repeat what you think you heard for confirmation or validation. Pause. Don't get ready to ask the next probing question. Just listen! The other guy's confirmation helps to put the matter to rest so that you can tackle the next point. Another theory about asking for affirmation is that repeated agreements set the stage for continued agreements. It's to your advantage to get the opponent into the habit of agreeing with you.

Next time you're at the bookstore, you may want to buy a book on the art of negotiation. You'll find a big selection of titles. It's obviously a subject that attracts broad interest and with good reason.

Doesn't Life Get In The Way?

Once you know what you want to achieve, how do you keep that vision front and center as time moves on? Practice!

Master the strategies that assist you to perfect this chapter's dynamite quartet — **Courage, Accountability, Deciding What You Want To Do And Knowing That Your Strengths Support That Goal,** and **Envisioning What Will Happen** — and you automatically place yourself in the fast lane to success.

STEP 3:
Develop Your Plan

Now that you have set your goals and envisioned what will happen, it's time to develop your action plan. You must first acquire relevant knowledge. Then you will determine the resources, relationships, strategies, and timelines required to achieve your goals.

Mr. Shakespeare added to our appreciation of the meaning of the word "knowledge" when he wrote, **"Ignorance is the curse of God; Knowledge, the wing wherewith we fly to heaven."**

Your depth of knowledge, general and specific, helps you participate in conversations and build relationships. It's likely that no one ever suggested to you that one reason to attain knowledge is to build relationships, but it's true. If you know nothing about nothing, it's really hard to carry on a conversation!

Pockets Of Knowledge

The knowledge you acquire fits into different categories. One level of knowledge is the knowledge you acquire about your work. Did you ever notice, for example, when you enter a Home Depot store that the people there know where the products are? They know what they have and what they don't have. They know how to help you locate what you're looking for. If a person working at Home Depot didn't have that knowledge, he or she wouldn't be of much use. I always admire a person who really understands the business he or she is in, no matter what that business is.

Another level of knowledge is general knowledge. A person should know about politics, world affairs, geography, history, and sports. These are all things that help to facilitate conversation. *It's through conversation that you build relationships and through relationships that you make connections that help you to grow and help you to grow your business.* I've met so many people in my career who had multiple degrees from the best universities in the country, and they had become so obsessed with where they got the degrees and what their knowledge level was that they missed the whole point – *you can't do it all by yourself.*

Still another level of knowledge is what you know about people and tendencies that people have, how they react to different things. You can study and read about behaviors but you need experience to supplement that information.

Illustration: I was in an interview once, and this was not that long ago. As a matter of fact, it was the interview for my final job. The interview lasted one hour and 27 minutes, and it was with the chief financial officer of the company. "Tell me about your high school years." I went through my high school years and college years and why I chose college, why I chose the major, why I chose my first job, why I left. Why? Why? Why? "Why do you think you're the right candidate for this job? Why this job right now?"

At the very end, he said, "I notice that you never mentioned that you had an MBA." I said, "That's true." He asked, "Why didn't you mention that?" I said, "Well, you never asked me. I answered all the questions that you asked. You never asked me about the MBA and that's why I didn't mention it."

I'm reasonably sure that often it's what you leave out that makes the biggest impression upon someone you want to impress!

Illustration: Some three to six months after I had been promoted into a new job, I had a consultant working with me. I really wanted to get some things moving rapidly. I had a series of meetings with my staff. The consultant interviewed me and she interviewed my staff. She gave me feedback from these interviews. We were supposed to talk from 5:00 P.M. until maybe 6:30 P.M. At 9:00 P.M., we were still talking. I finally said, "Why do I get the feeling that I'm the only person around here who cares about getting things accomplished?"

She looked at me and said, "Have you ever thought maybe they don't know how?" That had never crossed my mind because I assumed they were in the position and, therefore, knew what they were doing and that if they didn't produce or deliver a particular thing, it was because they chose not to do it. The thought that they didn't know how to accomplish things never crossed my mind.

From that day forward, I would always consider whether a person chose not to do something or didn't know how to do it. If a person didn't know how to do it, there was an opportunity to discuss that. I would set the stage for them to feel comfortable to talk about it and we would work through it. People find different ways to protect themselves. One way is to stall and delay and hope it goes away. Wait until somebody else does it and see how that person makes out. People develop different tactics because they don't want to reveal a weakness. To learn that people did this far more than I ever thought was an eye-opening experience.

Speaking of learning more about peoples' responses, I was at the same job, still relatively new, and I sent out requests to members of my team. We were in the same city, but in different buildings, and there were large numbers of people, clients, and issues to accommodate. Weeks would go by before I received responses. One day, in frustration, I said to my secretary, "I don't understand why it takes so long to respond to these requests." She said very softly, "Have you thought about putting a date on them — please respond by . . . ?"

I was operating under the assumption that people would work this into their schedules and get information to me as soon as possible. Apparently because I didn't supply a date, people procrastinated. They'd wait until I called them. My secretary taught me an excellent lesson!

Tell Me More, Tell Me More

Seminar attendance, discussion group participation, and continuing education courses can help fill your pockets of knowledge. I always caution people about one thing though: don't go out and take everything that's available whether it's applicable or not. Be selective. Here are some on-the-job learning experiences that are difficult to top. Let's have a drum roll, if you please. This information deserves it!

Staff Job

One of the things I learned about staff jobs is that your number one task is to be at the disposal of the head of that staff. And when you come in each day, your number one priority is whatever that person wants! Staff jobs are different because your whole purpose to be there is to make life easy for the person who is the head of staff. That's why the person has a staff.

Understanding that difference makes it a lot easier for the person in that position primarily because he or she is going to get interruption after interruption after interruption. When you get an interruption, put it in perspective. How does this request stack up in importance against what I'm doing now? If it's a greater or equal priority, why not set aside what I'm doing and take care of it and then come back to what I'm doing?

View interruptions as distractions that can be managed. Take time to understand concerns. Find out what's needed. If it's something that's needed tomorrow or next week, then make a note, which you'll refer to later, and continue working on matters at hand.

I've always believed that if you're focused and anything gets in your way (e.g., person or situation), you should view it as a distraction. Rarely will it be something so challenging that it could cause you to turn away from focusing on your goal. Another reason to view interruptions as distractions is so you can mentally minimize things that are getting in your way. The issues may be major, minor, and everything in between, but they're all distractions.

Managing A Staff And Scanning For Green Monsters

I always tried to keep a little humor in my organization and on my team. When someone would come to visit me with a proposal, or if I requested that someone take care of a particular task on my behalf, I wanted to rule out potential problems from the get-go. My way of communicating that was to say, "Okay, let's do it that way, but make sure that I don't have any green monsters camping outside of my door." Everybody in the organization knew they should keep an eye out for potential problems and jump on them fast should they appear.

Occasionally, I would ask, "Is there a monster in the woods?" I really wanted to know, "Have you done your homework? Have you really done your research? Is this problem bigger than you're telling me it is?"

Monsters Kicking Up Their Heels

When someone came into my office and told me not to worry, I'd think to myself — are you sure? I'd ask, "Did you find the monster or did you find the leg of the monster?" My staff knew they shouldn't wait until that green monster got big enough to be seen above the trees! At that point, I didn't need to ask questions because, if there's a monster out there (i.e., a big problem), people call me. If I get letters from clients, then the monster is above the trees.

The people who worked with me were up close and familiar with specific operations. *They lived in the woods!* If green monsters were encroaching on their territory, they would be the first to notice. I never wanted to see the monster kicking his heels above the trees because, if you identify problems when they're small, they're easier to fix. This spoon-full-of-sugar type message helped the medicine go down! The sighting of *green monsters* set off alarms. If you would like to put my green monsters to work for you, be my guest!

Twenty-Four Hours A Day

Here's one more bit of knowledge that comes to you direct from on-the-job learning experiences. . . . If we seek the perfect world, either at home or at work, we're going to waste time because nothing is perfect. If you accept the concept that you can't "fix" all the people you don't like, and you can't solve all the problems in the world, then the question is: "What shall you do despite the distractions?" There will always be distractions.

I had about seventeen bosses in my career — good ones, bad ones, and everything in between. My attitude was "don't sweat the small stuff." They were distractions. If something got to be more than a distraction and I couldn't handle it, then I would consider looking for another job. Assuming all the other things that I thought I should be getting out of the job were present, I wouldn't allow that to cause me to leave.

Take this idea one step farther. The person who seeks the perfect world won't find it. If you're not seeking the perfect world and you can accept that there will be distractions, you'll view them as normal – just a pattern of life. You won't waste time focusing on a difficult boss.

Listen carefully. Observe. Perform so that you please your boss as best you can. Sometimes nothing you do will suit your leader. At one meeting, my leader was attempting to answer a question and he was told to shut up, "I want Danny to answer the question."

It shouldn't surprise you to learn that tensions run high when billions of dollars are on the line, and the most refined people who generally display the best manners will dispense with them. Don't get rattled. Never go to a meeting thinking you're a tag-along. Just because your boss and other senior people are in attendance, don't assume anyone is going to shield you. If the going gets tough, the tough sometimes *duck*, too!

5

ON STAGE AND IN THE SPOTLIGHT

Success attributes that are widely acknowledged as common to all successful people are presented below. I don't believe there is one single thing that a person can do to become successful. I think it requires multiple things. You have to be a package, if you will, an integrated package. It's exciting to recognize that you can develop each of these attributes and put them to use.

Since this chapter discusses success attributes that aren't a surprise to anyone, you will probably have formed some opinion about each of them. Even so, be ready to give them careful attention. You may want to pause after reading each opening statement to be sure that you appreciate the full meaning. In this hurry-up world we inhabit, it's not unusual to race ahead believing "I know that" when, in fact, you may not know that as well as you can know it.

Although each success attribute is covered in some detail, there's always something more to be considered. Don't forget to check the "Worth Reading!" list at the end of the book. Promise yourself that you'll read one or more of these titles or other books that help support your continuous improvement.

STEP 4:
Perform Like Your Career Depends On It

People judge you by how well you meet your commitments. We'll explore many of the behind-the-scenes aspects of performing up to expectations. The process begins with a clear understanding of what the expectations are and moves through the steps of prioritizing, assessing talent, delegating, and delivering the required results.

Performance

"Promises are not binding where the performance is impossible." A party named Paley is credited with this observation. No additional information is provided. No matter, I heartily agree with Paley (see: www.dictionary.com).

Preparation supports any fine performance. Preparation involves understanding the past, doing the research, acquiring the resources, assessing the talent, and laying out the timeline. Some people feel overwhelmed when facing what they dub an impossible workload. (Note Paley's apt comment above.) It's a good time to mention that all busy and successful people are always too busy. If you think you're too busy, you're probably in good company! Let's cut it down to size.

Skillful prioritizing enables you to operate smoothly. The more you delegate, the more you're able to get done. You're able to manage bigger projects, bigger organizations, bigger teams. Even when you run a one-person business, if you subcontract tasks, you're delegating. Taking inventory of needed resources is another up-front action step. Resources include budget, equipment, and personnel. What sets the most successful business people apart from the crowd? They do all of the above but not until they *assess required results and determine how performance impacts their immediate boss.*

It's essential to know what is expected! In order to do that you must:

1. Know the recipient. The recipient can be your supervisor, co-workers, clients, or customers. Once you know who the recipient is, you might actually interview that person to clarify written information (e.g., letter of instruction, contract) so that when you begin the job performance, you know all that's involved: written, unwritten, and implied.

2. Determine how your performance impacts your immediate boss. If your boss isn't the direct recipient of the services you're about to perform, it's essential that you balance the boss's expectations with the expectations of those who are expecting service from you. *What???*

You may want to read the preceding observation one more time. It's a subtle one and rarely mentioned. You wouldn't be the first person to experience rough going because the boss acted as an impediment to delivering what had to be delivered to a client.There may be a myriad of reasons why. Your boss may have a different agenda and delegate work to you even when the boss knows you'll have to bump work that's promised to the client. The boss's motives and actions are not within your control, but your performance success is aligned with your ability to read the boss. Sometimes success is even aligned with knowing how to get around the boss. If this sounds heretical, so be it. Admittedly, these are fighting words and worthy of inspection but then I would digress far from the topic of performance.

Perhaps, it's enough to suggest that the more you learn about dealing with difficult people, the better you're able to turn in a top performance. Note that two out of three illustrations listed below are specific to dealing with difficult people. Now, you're ready to plan the steps required to get from A to Z.

Determine Resource Requirements

People, budget allocation, equipment; a typical assignment will require all these and more. Dollars and equipment needs are usually easy to determine, but when you're excellent at selecting the right person for the job, you come out head and shoulders above the rest. The business of evaluating people is an ongoing process.

Successful people know that each person in an organization has a relative potential to contribute. Let's say you don't have much interaction with the person who handles the telephone. You work directly with the administrative assistant who is the telephone operator's boss. Nevertheless, you know something about the capabilities of both people, albeit you know more about the administrative assistant.

Moving Mountains

The person who has great ability to interact with and influence others can move mountains. A person who has little or no such ability can't punch his way out of a wet paper bag. People who interact well with others are the people to whom you delegate important tasks. On the other side of this equation is the realization that if you're a person who builds excellent relationships with colleagues and staff, you're going to be sought after when people higher up in the organization need to find the right person for the job. It brings to mind the cry: "Uncle Sam Needs You!"

Deliver The Goods!

All of the above is for naught if you don't deliver the goods. In order to make sure you deliver the goods, you'll want to put a *feedback mechanism* in place. Let's examine the feedback mechanism for the job-doer and the job-giver since each of them must deliver the goods, and you'll find yourself in one role or another at any given time.

Job-Doer

If you're the person who receives an assignment, it is a smart strategy to seek feedback on your progress from time to time, in order to test whether or not it is meeting expectations. You know all about requirements, but sometimes, through misinterpretation or a changing situation, adjustments must be made. By asking for feedback from the job-giver, you may open up opportunities to deliver even more than was initially expected. Exceeding expectations is standard operating procedure for people who are setting a brisk pace for business success!

Job-Giver

You're a *sitting duck* unless you establish and participate in an interim feedback loop. If things aren't progressing as planned, you don't want to find out about it at the zero hour. In effect, you'll be watching to see if the talent you selected is qualified for the job. People that don't feel confident don't typically want you to monitor works in progress. You're probably well on your way to delivering the goods when the lines of communication between you and those to whom you've delegated tasks are wide open.

As a matter of fact, in the illustration that follows, I instituted Open Communications Sessions that were held at least once a month. I updated everyone on progress and encouraged discussion by inviting questions pertaining to any aspect of the assignment. I shared my personal performance appraisal and revealed that there were gaps, things that I could improve. I took the opportunity to explain that it's okay to have gaps as long as you know what they are and that you're committed to working on them.

I believe that by admitting to having gaps, I set the stage for others to do likewise and, in the end, this worked to improve performance. I also used the Open Communications Sessions to recognize individuals for jobs well done. Sometimes this was in the form of praise in front of their peers. Sometimes we included monetary awards. These sessions proved to be so successful that other directors initiated them for their various work groups.

The following illustration offers you a glimpse of PER-FORMANCE in action when the stakes are high.

Illustration: This illustration was the subject of a feature article "Lucent's Winning CFO Team," in the July 1998 issue of *Management Accounting.* Permission to reprint was obtained and you can read the article in its entirety. (See page 149.) This example of outstanding performance excellence is summarized here.

Project: Project Quantum Leap

Goal: Operate financial services that measure up to the "best in class" companies. That meant Lucent's financial processes would have to measure up to 22 other large companies in various industries with revenues ranging from $5 billion to $90 billion and with financial staffs of up to 15,000 employees.

Challenges: Reduce the cost of operations, which were considerably greater than several "best in class" companies. Improve service to internal customers. (Lowering costs while improving services? Yes!)

Focus: Everyone is working toward costing the corporation no more than one percent of revenue received.

Timing: Lucent Technologies evolved from the company known as Western Electric and then AT&T Network Systems. It became a stand-alone company on October 1, 1996. The benchmarking process actually began in 1994-1995 prior to Lucent's emergence as a stand-alone company. The article in *Management Accounting* appeared in July 1998. So you know immediately that this was a long-term effort. Project Quantum Leap was in high gear for about three years.

Outcome: We reduced costs by 40 percent over a three-year period.

Status: When asked what key ingredients made Project Quantum Leap a success, I replied, "The commitment and sacrifices made by all Lucent Financial Services (LFS) colleagues, top-down measurable commitments, a willingness to learn from others, and the project-by-project approach to continuous process improvement." As you may recall, I was Director of Lucent Financial Services, and the *Management Accounting* writer used that statement to conclude his article. It's a performance that I'm enormously proud of and pleased to share with you.

Illustration: Here's a true story about handling difficult situations with peers. It was routine practice for the books to be closed at the end of each month. I was attending a meeting while a large team of people who worked with me was closing the books. Suddenly, one of the team came into the meeting room to get me. He reported that one of my peers was "transferring a $30 million negative variance to us in the middle of the book-closing process." (A negative variance refers to an expense you didn't anticipate.)

Now, my immediate boss was away participating in an executive education course for about six weeks, and I was in charge. I phoned my peer and he told me, "We have to do this. I spoke to my vice president and he agrees that we have to make this adjustment." I told him, "I don't know if you realize my boss is away for six weeks and I'm acting for him. That means the only person I'm accountable to is the president of the unit. I don't want to play one-upmanship with you, but I can tell you we can't accept this $30 million variance. I'll have to go directly to the president about it because you're not giving me any choice." To make a long story short, I got a call back 30 minutes later to tell me, "We're withdrawing the $30 million variance."

When the going gets tough, the tough use the resources at their disposal. In this case, the only resource at my disposal happened to be a good one.

Let me add that a few days later I was in a meeting, still representing my boss, and sitting about three seats down from me was the vice president who was involved in the "almost" transaction. I didn't know how much my peer had told him about me and what had transpired or why he had chosen to back down, even though I had a good idea as to why. When we had a break, everybody stood up to leave the room and I had two options. One option was to exit as fast as I could. The other was to be proactive. I walked right up to him, shook his hand, and said, "Thank you for your support last week."

Illustration: A security manager had a staff of 18 to 20 security officers and a secretary. He believed in having his own vacation policy that was separate from the company policy. He had many other rules that I later learned about but this one comes to mind. One day, one of the security guards apparently gave a copy of the internal memo with the local vacation policy on it to the secretary and asked her to drop it off in my office.

Well, I confronted the manager about the document, and he looked shocked and surprised that I had a copy. I discussed with him how it's not appropriate to have a separate vacation policy. He made statements like, "We're different; we need to protect the people. We need to make sure that we have sufficient coverage." He had a whole list of reasons. But at the end of the discussion, I told him it's still inappropriate and please "make it go away." He agreed.

Two days later, as I was passing his office on my way to lunch, he called to me. "Danny, come in. I think I've solved the problem." I stepped into his office and he said, "I know who gave you this memo." I said, "That was not the task." He said, "My secretary gave you this memo. Let me tell you how I know."

He proceeded to tell me how he figured out that his secretary gave me the memo. I did not confirm where I got the memo but repeated to him, "That is not what I asked you to do."

About an hour later, his secretary came to my office, crying. She thought I had told where I got the memo. As a matter of fact, he told her that I told him so. She admitted to me that he threatened to fire her if she did anything like that again. I told her exactly what I told you. He spent two days investigating to find out who gave me that memo, rather than getting rid of the policy. And he figured it out. That was his specialty. He prided himself on being like J. Edgar Hoover. He said, "I don't call people and ask them what they've been doing. I call them in and I tell them what they've been doing."

I went to see this manager. I told him that his actions were inappropriate. He should never have confronted this woman about having delivered that memo to me. And he should have immediately discarded the policy and dropped the issue. I explained to him that what he had done was to destroy the confidence of his secretary and further intimidate the people who report to him because they now know that she got caught, so they'll probably never send another memo about this. I also told him I had to document what occurred and, finally, I informed him that disciplinary action would be taken.

You really have to monitor an individual who operates like this. You have to make sure that you're involved in what they're doing. If you go off and get busy with other things, it just gives them opportunity to "get off the ranch again." One of the guards told me that the security manager had forbidden her to practice parachuting over the weekend. "I believe this is my personal time," she said to me.

Apparently, this guy had been allowed to do anything he wanted to do up until that time. When it was announced that he was going to be reporting to me, everybody was waiting to see what would happen.

On the other hand, this guy was the one that sat in my office through a bomb threat! On one level, you know this person prides himself on being right. "I don't ask you what's going on. I tell you." He told me, "Danny, it's a hoax." It was. The fact that someone in his position had been permitted to function with his own set of rules for so long provided him with a comfort zone. When it came to security matters, he was an expert. I made no secret of monitoring human resource matters in his department. He knew I respected his record of excellence when it came to security matters. And we moved forward.

Five Worksheets You Can Use To Help You

Worksheets entitled *Deal with Difficult People, Prioritize, Delegate Tasks, Take Inventory of Resources,* and *Deliver the Required Result* are provided following page 61. They're presented as models or patterns, much like tailors' patterns. Use any one of them as you find it, alter it, or start looking for a pattern you like better.

Commitment Plays A Key Role

Commitment is closely aligned with performing like your career depends on it. Synonyms, such as responsibility, obligation, and duty, help to define the word "commitment."

> "To John I owed great obligation; But John, unhappily, thought fit to publish it to all the nation: Sure John and I are more than quit." (Matthew Prior, 1718).

The story is brief. The impact is profound.

How you respond to a commitment that you make tells others a lot about you. You're either dependable or undependable. The person or persons on the receiving end are impacted by your actions. Sometimes the stakes are high and sometimes they're not. Nevertheless, you become the kind of person other people are attracted to when you're perceived to be dependable and, therefore, you must always honor commitments. Of course, you can over-commit or under-commit. Oops! What then? The following information enables you to prevent or cope with either of the above. As you maximize your potential to get what you want from your career, you get a not surprising bonus in the bargain. You favorably impact relationships with your spouse, family, friends, and others.

First-Half-of-The-Day Priorities

Prior to my retirement, I would think about the three or four most important things to be done the next workday. I didn't always write them down, but I had an idea of the most important thing to focus on. And that would get my attention in the first half of the day. If I got those things done, delegated, or set in motion, then I had time in the afternoon to engage in other day-to-day things, but those priorities would come first.

Caution Sign Ahead!

You're in a meeting and you're asked, "When can you get A or B for me?" It may work sometimes to say, "I don't know. I'll check with my team and get back to you." But often you have to be familiar enough with your team and with your team's capabilities to give an estimate with some extra time built in to give your team some flexibility. You wouldn't want to commit constantly to things that your team is not capable of delivering. Assessing commitments is simply something one has to do.

Once you get into it, if you do find that you've overestimated your team's delivery capability, then you have an obligation to go back and negotiate a different date. That's not something you want to do often either. You want to maintain a good track record and keep your reputation intact.

There are times when you assess an assignment as best as you can but discover it's going to be difficult to keep promises. If you're essentially the only one committed to the task, you're at liberty to find a way to make it work!

An Impossible Trip

I'll tell you about a trip I made that people said was not possible. I was asked to be in Washington, D.C., for two months. At the time, I had already committed to a set of dates to be in Brazil and Argentina. The Washington assignment was going to conflict with that to some extent. I accepted the Washington assignment, which meant I had to be in D.C. on a Wednesday night for a kick-off meeting pertaining to bargaining with the union and here's what I did. I left Atlanta on Sunday night, flew overnight to Brazil, had an all-day meeting the next day, went out to dinner that night, and got up the next morning and flew to Argentina. I had a meeting with the folks in Argentina and flew that night to Atlanta. I left Atlanta the following afternoon at 2:00 P.M. and arrived in Washington, D.C., for the kick-off meeting. All this took place between a Sunday night and a Wednesday and if you ask me why, I'll tell you in one word, commitment!

It was essential that I be alert and focused, and this I accomplished with a little help from my friends. I trusted the people I was going to visit. They selected the hotels. They arranged to have me picked up at the airports. As a matter of fact, in Argentina, the local Lucent manager came to the airport to meet me herself. So even though I was going to an unknown place and didn't speak the language, I was going to be with people I'd met before and could trust. As a result, I was able to use all my energies to focus on what I had to do.

Fortunately, I rarely got tired during these long flights and time zone changes. I remember another time when I was flying back from Europe, I stopped in the Netherlands for a meeting and took a morning flight home to Atlanta. I arrived in Atlanta about 2:00 P.M. and went to my office for a 3:15 P.M. meeting with a Lucent colleague who was Mexico-based but who would be in Georgia that day. He had some issues about his budget and wanted to meet with me. I made the commitment to meet with him and we met.

The Parking Space Caper

If you believe my actions were above and beyond the call of duty, may I suggest you also consider that those very same actions helped to cement my reputation. My reputation spoke volumes for me on countless occasions. To illustrate, let me tell you about the parking space caper!

After working as controller in our Dallas factory for about two years, my duties were expanded to include human resources, labor relations, and some other functions. Whenever my leader was out of town, I was in charge of all administrative functions, including security and the parking lot.

Approximately 3,000 people worked at this facility, so the parking lot was large. Managers had reserved parking spaces and, depending upon your level, your space was designated nearer to or farther from the building entrance.

The general manager had the closest spot, the second in command had the next spot, and so on and so forth. We had one company-owned car parked right between the general manager and the second in command. Well, my leader's secretary was getting older and it was becoming more difficult for her to walk the length of the parking lot. I don't know if she made the request or he made the offer but the company car was relocated, and the secretary was given the number two parking spot.

We had several engineering managers (one in particular) who didn't like that, and when the boss was away on a business trip, they approached me on a Friday afternoon. They told me they were going to paint the parking lot over the weekend. I asked, "Why are you telling me? Is this something you normally do?" They assured me it was and I said, "Okay. Lots of luck. See you Monday."

When they repainted the parking lot, they eliminated one space. When everyone came to work on Monday, guess what? There was no space next to the general manager's space. The spaces went from general manager to engineering manager, the second in command.

Well, the general manager was back. When his secretary arrived, she walked straight into his office and said, "I guess from now on, you're going to have to get accustomed to me arriving 15 minutes late, because it takes a long time to walk from the back side of the parking lot."

Naturally, he asked her what she was talking about and when he realized what had happened, he knew exactly who to look for. He knew that was something I wouldn't do! (The culprit was asked to return the missing space. He complied.)

Not The End Of The Story

The same person who made the parking space disappear wasn't comfortable with the fact that I was sitting in the front office because I didn't have the rank of the other two or three people in that office area. Even though I was the controller and reported to the head guy, in his view, I didn't belong in the front office.

One weekend, he moved my desk around the corner. When my boss came looking for me, he asked, "What are you doing around here?" I told him, "Someone moved my office over the weekend." Not only did he force the guy to move me back into the front office, he had to give me new wallpaper and new carpeting for my inconvenience.

Roasty, Toasty

Some of these pranks may seem funny. To me, having my office moved was merely a distraction. But the sum of a person's actions labels that person as someone who is dependable or undependable. When this joker retired, I was one of the roasters at his retirement party!

One of his pet peeves was not wanting anyone to use his parking space, even when he was out of town. He didn't like accountants taking sodas out of the refrigerator in the executive area. And he didn't hesitate to come across the hall to tell me what he thought a good controller should be like. So I made a list of his well-known pet peeves and said, "I really took your advice. I truly wanted to be a good controller and make sure the company didn't owe you any money. I went around and found everybody who parked in your parking space and charged them $5 apiece. I found everybody who took a soda from the executive office refrigerator and charged them $1. I added it all up and it came to $1,800, but I thought about it. You told me that I should always be accurate. So, I started checking and found that you owed this much and then I found that you owed . . . . And I got all the way down to $3.27 cents. So, here's your check for $3.27." (I handed him the check.)

I don't think anybody in the audience thought I'd have the courage to do that, and the laughter literally stopped the show. I never hesitated to add humor to the mix, when it was appropriate. " Appropriate" is the operating word!

A Wanted Man

I applied for only two of the approximately 15 jobs I had during my long business career. I uncovered the power of being the kind of person others are attracted to as I made a serious effort to learn why everyone around me applied for this job, applied for that job. Will you apply for your next job or will someone come and say, "We want you?" It's good to be wanted! As you set the pace for business success, being wanted follows naturally, much like night follows day. Having said that, let me add that you may feel as though you've been on the job for a long time and nothing is happening. "I've been doing this. I've been doing that. Everyone else is getting ahead." The fact is, time will go by quickly if you're doing all the things you need to do. In a large company, someone will be knocking on your door, wanting to promote you, and giving you even more responsibility before you've completed developing yourself and done what you want to do in the current job. So the way to make time go by fast and enjoy yourself more is to focus on self-improvement. Apply the steps we're discussing and you can't miss. You'll become the type of person who attracts others to you.

It may interest you to know I've been offered three to four unsolicited jobs since I retired. I did accept a teaching position with Tuskegee University during the Fall '99 semester in the College of Business and Organizational Management. At the end of that time, students completed a Student Evaluation of Classroom Instruction/Faculty Summary Profile. It was gratifying to discover that I was recognized as one of the most popular instructors. I share this information with you to underscore that the success attributes I espouse are the ones I still use. Although I'm retired, these steps continue to take me to "lofty" places.

DEAL WITH DIFFICULT PEOPLE

If you want a dictum to live by when it comes to working with difficult people, use mine: You can't fix everybody you don't like. You have to minimize the interruption. Minimize the interruption and continue. You may want to copy the few items listed under *A Strategy* and keep them within easy reach. Refer to them when dealing with difficult people.

A Strategy:
- Don't judge people until you have the facts. That means enter a situation with an open mind.
- Be willing to listen so that you can hear precisely what it is that concerns the other guy. You may not agree. You may know early in the conversation that you don't agree, but it's important to understand the facts involved and the perceptions this person entertains.
- Throughout the process, ask probing questions. Have you tried this? Have you tried that? What about this?

Many times, a difficult person will shoot down every option you offer but, in the process of going through the options, you'll be working to get to the heart of what's driving that person because sometimes it's not what's on the surface. It's necessary to get underneath and find out what's really "bugging" someone. Why is the person behaving the way he/she is behaving? What past experience caused this individual to be skeptical, confrontational, or what you may perceive to be difficult! (You may not be able to determine this but it's worth a try.)

- Keep the person focused. It's important to let the person know up front the approximate amount of time available for this conversation. That will probably cause the person to focus.

- Observe the person's behavior and discuss the behavior rather than the person. "I've observed this behavior, and I'd like you to discontinue the behavior, and I'm willing to discuss why this isn't acceptable behavior. Maybe there are options. Maybe we can remove the screw that's driving you to behave this way. But the behavior itself is not acceptable." (If someone else reported objectionable behavior, you may want to invite that person to be present.) And once we've gotten all the facts out, it's easier to talk about options.

The following exercise is for use by anyone. It supplies the questions. You supply the answers.

1. One person I think of as difficult is (name). Why is that? If I label this person "different," instead of "difficult," would my response be different, too?
2. Can I spend less time with difficult people? Is this "wish" a practical one? Do I feel better just thinking about controlling the time I spend with difficult people?
3. What happens to me when I'm with difficult people? Do I feel angry? Do I stop listening? Do I ever stop to think about what makes the other person tick? Would I feel differently if I knew difficult people were worried, ill informed, feeling stressful? In other words, if I recognize someone's vulnerabilities, would I perceive that person to be less of an irritant?
4. Am I a calm person? Do I grimace and use body language that sends a negative message to people who annoy me? Can I fine-tune my behavior to encourage others to behave better? One way to do that is. . . .
5 Can I quietly observe someone who seems to get along well with everyone? Can I learn by observing what it is he or she does that I don't do?

Here are three steps that I can put into action. I'll concentrate on them for one week and then take ten minutes to write out an evaluation. I'll repeat the process the following week and compare my written evaluations. This may offer clues to better ways to proceed. I realize that if one strategy isn't effective, another one will be. I'll continue to work on sharpening my skills.

1. Spend less time with anyone I consider difficult. Be polite but firm. Let the person know in advance, I'm busy. (Then, get busy!) "Sam, I'd enjoy hearing more about your casino winnings but my boss needs these figures in one hour."

2. Imagine that someone has come to me for advice about how to deal with a difficult person.. What advice would I give? (Now, take your own advice and try it.)

3. Monitor my body language. Smile more often. Maintain good posture. Make eye contact during conversation. Walk briskly. Send a message of professionalism. (Others may respond in a no-nonsense professional manner. Now, the stage is set to get on with the business of business.)

This photo was taken in 1956 at my grandparents' farm, where we lived from 1953 until 1967. From Left to Right: my brothers Harry and Sam and me. In the back row: my Aunt Evelyn, holding my cousin Yvonne, and my mother, Mabel.

Me, after my college graduation ceremony at Tuskegee University in 1971.

My brothers with me at my home in July 1999. From left to right: Harry, me, Sam, and Timmy.

A night out with my wife, Rose.

My son, Danny, Jr., with me in Tampa, Florida, for Superbowl XXXV.

Busy at work in my office in 1999.

*Presenting an award to an employee for
a cost-saving suggestion in 1998.*

Singing "Sitting on the Dock of the Bay" at a diversity celebration in 1998.

Visiting Karin Lin of Lucent's China financial operations in January 1999.

WORKSHEET 2
PRIORITIZE

When you've got something that must be done, give it the POW test:

P — PRESSING. On a scale of 1 - 5, with 1 serving as the most pressing, assign the task a numerical value.

O — ORDER. Now, you're ready to assign the task a time and place to be tackled.

W — WATCH STATUS. Monitor progress.

This is a quick and simple approach to prioritizing. You may already be using the POW technique and haven't thought about it in these terms. It can be comforting to recognize that there's a systematic approach to achieving goals and it works!

Do It Now

Whenever a task needs attention, and you can interrupt what you're doing and give it immediate attention, do it! It saves time if you can:

- Accept a telephone call instead of having to return the call.
- See someone who arrives at your office unannounced.
- Originate a call you've been asked to make and notify the party who asked you to do so of the outcome.
- Dictate or write a short memo.
- Read printed material delivered to your desk (e.g., reports, mail), and discard or route it accordingly.

Draw the Line

On Monday, you had six tasks that merited the POW test. By Friday morning, you're handling nine pressing tasks.

1. Ask how much is too much? If pressing tasks commonly tend to escalate rather than diminish, operations may need to be reviewed. Unless you're working in a hospital emergency room, where hectic activity is normal, a steady, large number of urgent matters may signal weak links in your area. (Check Worksheet 4: Take Inventory of Resources.) Consider delegating or renegotiating deadlines. Set realistic deadlines from the get-go.

2. Make time for recording *pressing* activities for one or two weeks. You may find that you handle six to nine to twelve priorities as assignments with ease. If you do, you should know it! You won't mistakenly assume that you're running on overload. In that case, there's no need to draw the line!

Document Activity

1. Maintain a "to-do" list on an electronic or paper calendar or an appropriate tracking device. Choose a method that suits your style. Theoretically, if you embrace this tool, you'll use it! Regular updates are necessary so that information is always dependable.

2. Avoid using this tool! The rationale is that if you **do it now**, you won't have to track tasks.

WORKSHEET 3
DELEGATE TASKS

In order to manage large groups of people, complicated projects, or bigger assignments, it's necessary to delegate tasks. To make it easier for you, this worksheet is designed to bolster your personal comfort zone. Remember, anyone can assign tasks to others, but you want to practice the fine art of delegation while remaining in your personal comfort zone. (After all, the goal is to assist you to set the pace for business success. You can perform better from within your comfort zone.) Feel free to customize this worksheet. If you add steps, ask: How does this benefit me? If it doesn't benefit you. . . forgetaboutit!

1. When possible, divide a priority into a four-part project.

Illustration: *Task:* Interview Chris Jones and write a safety-first article for the employee newsletter.

Break-out:

(1) Contact Chris Jones and secure a time slot to conduct an interview.

(2) Obtain facts about Chris Jones's credentials and about the company's safety record

(3) Prepare a list of questions and conduct the interview

(4) Write the article.

Put a checkmark next to each part you *don't* have to handle.

Illustration: Perhaps you know Chris Jones personally and feel it's appropriate to secure the interview time slot with him. You'll rest easier knowing that the interview will take place in a timely fashion so the deadline can be met. Someone else can do the preliminary research, conduct the interview, and write the article.

2. Use a share-the-load approach.

Illustration: Employee A tends to be detail oriented but can't write well. Employee B, on the other hand, is a fine communicator but she's scheduled to be off-site to attend a training session for the next two weeks. Ask Employee A to obtain background information. Employee B can conduct the interview and write the article when she returns.

3. Know your customer!

A stockbroker invites trouble if he or she foists a risky product line on a customer who is a demonstrated conservative investor. You'll avoid trouble if you know about the abilities of anyone whose aid you want to enlist.

There's More

A moment ago, I referred to the fine art of delegation. No one is proficient in any of the fine arts without practice. Don't be discouraged if early delegation assignments you make leave you up the proverbial creek. You'll get better at delegating. From time to time, you'll come across how-to-delegate information. Whether it's in an article in a business magazine, a topic offered in a seminar setting, or an entire book about delegation you find in the library, learn from it.

By the way, delegation always involves more than one. One asks and one (or many) respond. Don't mess with this equation. If someone asks you to do something and you can do it, cooperate. Turn in a dynamite performance. In time, many folks will feel as though they "owe you one." That's nice. It could mean you've got lots of people who really want to help you when you need help.

WORKSHEET 4
TAKE INVENTORY OF RESOURCES

First, Identify Resources Needed

- Make a wish list.
- Whittle it down, based upon reality (e. g., four staff members would be ideal but you have only two staff members).
- Play "what if" (e.g., What if you could "borrow'" two additional staff members from another department for a defined period of time?).

Did You Remember To Assess?

- Budget (i.e., dollars)
- Time required
- Skilled personnel available
- Supplier or vendor cooperation
- Seasonal considerations (e.g., weather)
- Time conflicts (e.g., scheduled vacation, prepaid convention attendance)
- Space availability (i.e., warehouse space, meeting rooms)
- Materials required (i.e., soft goods, hard goods)
- Transportation vehicles for goods or personnel
- Delivery consideration, such as time required to literally transport goods.

Add It Up

Don't begin your project until you have a complete understanding of required and available resources. By assuming that some resources aren't available, you begin the project with your eyes wide open. No surprises. You've got time on your side to obtain the missing items.

If what's missing is critical to operations, notify your boss or the appropriate party immediately. You may have to renegotiate a deadline, and the sooner you do this, the better for all concerned.

Taking "No" For An Answer

Why take "no" for an answer when you can circumvent challenges and move on?

Consider the following:

- "Borrow" personnel from other departments
- Hire temporary personnel from an agency
- Extend work hours for a fixed period of time
- "Bump" a job in progress that has a lower priority or a later deadline date
- Invite recently retired people who have needed skills to return to work for a defined period of time
- If your vendor can't supply you, can you use another vendor? Can you requisition materials from other departments?
- If you're needed in two places at once, what then? Is teleconferencing an option?
- Is there someone you can rely upon (e.g., a coach, a mentor) for constructive input as you assess pros and cons? If so, ask for it!

In short, think out of the box, and you may not have to take "no" for an answer!

WORKSHEET 5
DELIVER THE REQUIRED RESULT

This is the shortest worksheet of all. It's arguably the most important one!

(1) What is the purpose of the assignment?
(2) Who benefits from the assignment?
(3) How does this work impact your leader?

After you answer these questions, you'll be better able to answer this one: What is the required result?

Illustration: An executive asks for detailed financial breakdowns. You know he's using them for forecasting purposes and can accomplish his goal with approximate figures. You can deliver approximate figures in less than half the time it would take to produce complete financial breakdowns. He wants the figures delivered in 48 hours. You've been told to keep costs down in your department. Your leader doesn't want you to approve overtime work. Once you know the purpose of the assignment, who benefits, and how it impacts your leader, you realize you can deliver the required result. In this case, it means providing approximate figures. It's not what the executive asked for but it's what he needs. This strategy enables you to please more people more often. Unearth the desired result before you begin any project! It's unnecessary to deliver more.

By the way, mindreader talents, which help you to recognize what's needed, are in excellent working order when you're a careful listener and when you understand your business.

A Warning

I don't advocate doing anything less than exceeding expectations. Be aware that *Delivering the Required Result* usually allows you to meet or exceed anyone's expectations. No matter whether you're doing something to service internal or external customers, you'll want to answer all three questions before you proceed. Identify the required result and get started.

STEP 5:
Surround Yourself With People Who "Make A Positive Difference"

No one succeeds alone. As you develop relationships at work, at home, and in the community, it's important to seek people who share your passion for success. Ally with people who don't waste your time, test your spirit, or let you down at a critical moment. Find people who have strengths that you don't have. Team with people who share your values and will support you in achieving your goals.

"You Can Learn From Positive People" is the title of the second chapter in the book, *Projecting a Positive Image* (New York: Barron's, 1993). Author Marilyn Pincus writes:

> Pull positive thinkers into your circle. It's not difficult to locate bad news. It's the stuff they use to spin headlines. Office gossips spread it thick and fast. . . . Bad news is not what you hear when the coach gives a pep talk, when the salesperson comes to tout a new product or when your spouse wants to buy a new sports car and you're dreaming of a touring model.
>
> The coach, salesperson, and your spouse may be positive thinkers, or they may be using positive arguments in order to rise to the occasion. It's important to take note of that distinction when you look around to locate positive people. They're the ones who generally enjoy a positive outlook all the time. They don't pump the plus side of an argument simply to further their goals: they see the plus side of things as a matter of course.
>
> Moreover, these positive people have good judgment, inspire you with their logical reasoning, and are very much in touch with reality as you perceive it..
>
> Grab those folks! Pull them into your circle. They make it easier for you to stay on track . . . .

Illustration: At one point in my career, I was managing about 1,500 people and was initially overwhelmed trying to decide how to go about managing such a large group. I knew I had to rely heavily on the structure that was in place, but at the same time, I had to have my own avenues for reaching the masses. We had different group meetings and different recognition sessions where people were lauded for various achievements.

The district managers would organize these gatherings and invite me to attend. So being an invited speaker within my own organization two or three times a week wasn't unusual. Apparently, that "image" of me took hold. One day when I arrived to attend a luncheon with 200 other people, I looked at the printed program and s-u-r-p-r-i-s-e I learned I was the keynote speaker! Obviously, it was assumed that I just do this stuff; I didn't have to prepare.

Conjecture

People make assumptions all the time. Don't you? You have it within your power to send messages about yourself that you want to send. I don't know that I wanted people to think of me as such a competent speaker that I didn't need to be notified in advance that I was the keynote speaker, but it was a flattering assumption. Which raises another point: You knowingly or unknowingly send messages all the time. Since you're *Setting the Pace for Business Success,* you overlook a golden opportunity to put yourself in the fast lane if you don't utilize this knowledge.

Stick With It

It takes time to build relationships, and in this "instant" world we inhabit, where most people want things accomplished yesterday, the value of applying stick-to-itive-ness often goes unnoticed. Relationships you'll build with people who will help you and people you'll help typically take time to develop.

I was especially impressed by a business friend of mine who stuck it out when he had every reason to think he wasn't appreciated and should go elsewhere.

Illustration: This friend and I were peers and he was demoted. He felt crushed. Soon afterward, he happened to be in Atlanta on a business trip and called me and we went to dinner together. We spent three hours talking about what had happened to him and why he thought it happened and what he should do next. I listened. I encouraged him to *stay positive.*

I assured him I had the same level of respect for him that I had always had and thought he was a capable manager and still had a good future. After two years, this guy regained his level, moved on to accept an international assignment, and was recently promoted again. So he's now at a level higher than the level he had before he was demoted, he's well respected, and he has attained "lofty" goals.

As I share this story with you, you may have noticed that I was there to act as a sounding board for this person and to spotlight *believing in positive outcomes.* I was also able to help him discuss options when his thinking may have been cluttered because he was so close to what was happening. After he gave me a few of the facts, I was able to assist him to identify and sort a wide range of possible options. He contacted me because he knew something about me and perhaps knew I would level with him. I was in his network.

Put Together Your Network

It's natural to develop networks at work, at home, in the community. Step 5 (Surround Yourself With People Who "Make A Positive Difference") alerts you to doing so in a non-haphazard fashion. We all have to spend time with people who we don't expect to make "a positive difference" but you can hold that time to a minimum.

When it comes to maximizing your potential to get

what you want, you realize the value of putting together this network carefully and ceaselessly. You know that you will offer those who are within your network everything you can to help them maximize their potential to get what they want!

The Amazing Secretary

I didn't have a secretary until later in my career, and I learned the value of a secretary when I had the first one who didn't "make a positive difference."

Illustration: One week ahead of time, I asked for airline tickets to fly to Atlanta from New Jersey. I was given assurances that tickets would be ready for me. About two hours before I was to leave for the airport, I asked for the tickets. My secretary asked "What tickets?"

I made the trip. I also made my own arrangements to get there!

Soon afterward, I was promoted to the job where I had responsibility for 1,500 people. The secretary who was assigned to work with me was experienced, respected, and actually served as a coach to other secretaries. If I made a request, I could totally depend on her to make arrangements or contact people. She was very pleasant on the telephone, and whenever people needed to contact me, she would find ways to accommodate them. In short, she was amazing and appreciated!

The Dynamics

My last three amazing secretaries:
- Were mature and experienced
- Were well-informed
- Trusted me and I trusted them
- Had a good sense of humor
- Were flexible — ready to do almost anything asked. (If a task wasn't work-related [e.g., making my dental appointment], I didn't ask.)

- Were considerate
- Were my good partners

I always encouraged my secretaries, my assistants, and everybody on my team to take advantage of any opportunity. When I had amazing secretaries, I didn't want to lose them. But I asked myself what was worse: to hold someone back or to find someone else to fill the position? I don't think it's wise to hold people back from pursuing their goals.

Illustration: When I returned to work in Atlanta, after being away for five years, I ultimately rehired Jan, my former secretary. According to company rules, I had to post the job and interview several people. At one point, she came to me and asked if I was going to interview her. Of course! Two months after I hired her, she came to me to announce her retirement.

I told her, "I think that's great." (Obviously, this wasn't good timing as far as I was concerned.) I asked, "Who should your replacement be?" In fact, I asked for three recommendations. If, by some remote chance, the "chemistry" wasn't right with one person, I wanted options available to me. Patti, the woman my secretary favored, was hired and she lived up to my expectations. I asked my secretary to stay until Patti was trained. She agreed and the transition was smooth.

Executive Assistants

Dona, the executive assistant who worked with me, had responsibility for budgets, communication and public relations matters, planning meeting agendas, and acting as an interface between managers and human resources.

Good chemistry is essential. Also, if you're not a detail person, and I'm not, the executive assistant had better excel at taking care of details. She did.

In short, your secretary and executive assistant should be people who epitomize Step 5 in practice.

STEP 6:
Utilize "Exposure" For All It's Worth

To be successful, you have to go where the action is. Whether it's at headquarters or in Hollywood, you must gain exposure to people who are already doing what you want to do. You will learn from them, and they are in the best position to help you with your career.

I had an opportunity to transfer from Atlanta to New Jersey early in my career. New Jersey is the home of AT&T and Lucent Technologies Corporate Headquarters. Before I arrived, I was told this job would allow me "exposure" but I wasn't fully aware of what that meant. Once I was there, I had so many opportunities to meet people who were my peers as well as people who were at higher levels in the organization. Many of these people were going to move up to very responsible positions in the corporation and some of the people already were in those positions. This opportunity affected the rest of my working career. I can trace that early exposure to people that I met that I never knew and never would have known — people who got to know me, see me in action, and who acted on my behalf in the years to come.

Illustration: I had worked at a factory location and knew the operation of a factory accounting group. That experience lead to my being promoted and assigned to Dallas to be the controller at the Dallas factory. Three years into my Dallas tour, I was attending a meeting in New Jersey and was speaking with a director whom I had gotten to know when I had originally worked in New Jersey. He asked me about my job in Dallas and asked if I'd be interested in coming back to New Jersey. Now, if I hadn't gone to that particular meeting, or if he didn't already know me from a previous time, he might not have inquired about me and what I was doing. So there are links back to the people to whom you're exposed early in your career. And those people follow your career. If you're there (exposed), you become more real than if you are somewhere at a distance and people only know about you on paper.

Illustration: Nelson, the man that I coached and mentored and who went on to enjoy a long and successful career, was from North Carolina. He went to New Jersey to the corporate office. When I was transferred there from Dallas, I met him. Had he not transferred from North Carolina, I wouldn't have met him.

Illustration: We were living in Dallas and became friendly with people who lived around the corner from us. One day, this neighbor asked for my opinion about moving to California. His local office had closed and he was temporarily out of work. He and his wife were trying to decide if he should consider a job far away from Dallas. They both had been born and raised in Dallas and were concerned about leaving family, friends, the usual things.

I told him that Rose and I had similar concerns the first time we moved from Atlanta to New Jersey. There was some learning related to the process, but we made new friends and things worked out. As a matter of fact, our move to Dallas was our second relocation. Since our neighbors had always been "local" people, the chance of our meeting would have been non-existent if Rose and I didn't move to Dallas. I mention this because, after all these years, we're still good friends.

If I Knew Then What I Know Now

The first two times Rose and I moved, she had to leave her jobs and find new ones. The first time, she managed to find a job after about six weeks but the second time it took six months. And it was a job that paid less money. But then, I got wiser. I made her job a condition of my transfer. So, if we couldn't arrange a comparable job — I want to emphasize the word "comparable" — the deal was off. Rose and I decided we were willing to live with that arrangement, whatever it meant. It came to pass that Rose accepted jobs in different parts of the same company I worked for and saying "no" to a transfer was never an issue.

Where's The Action?

Did you ever notice that people who are in the entertainment business tend to migrate to New York or California because that's where the action is? Going to where the company headquarters is located is like going to Hollywood if you are a movie star. You can be discovered, nurtured, given opportunities. That's why exposure is so important.

I recommend that if you're working for a large corporation and have the opportunity to do a tour at the corporate headquarters, even if it's just for two years, it can make all the difference because in that two-year period, you'll meet a lifetime of associates and coaches, sponsors, and friends.

(Note: If you work in a small company or operate as an independent contractor, Step 6 relates to you, too. You're likely to find the "action" when you become active in professional organizations, chambers of commerce, and outside organizations where you're "exposed" to people you can learn from and who are in the best position to help you with your career.)

In all situations, it's important to use "exposure" for the right reasons. You want to be discovered, nurtured, given opportunities. Since you're setting the pace for business success, it's essential that you don't act "pushy." You're more attractive to others when you aren't constantly scratching and looking for that next job. People wonder, "Why is this person so aggressive? Why does she want to get away from her job?" Instead of having people ask: "What's going on?" offer them an opportunity to become impressed with you. Send a message of self-confidence. Being "pushy" sends the opposite message!

A Sense Of Timing

Timing can work for you or against you. If you take a job assignment that happens to put you in a place where a vacancy becomes available and you are in the vicinity, are available, and have the skills, you may have an edge on the person who has comparable skills but is not at that location. And that may result in your being selected for a particular job. Another way timing can work for you is when you've been on an assignment and a vacancy comes up at a higher level. You're already there working with this team and they've had an opportunity to see you in action. They haven't had an opportunity to see the other person in action, so it's exposure and timing blended together that can propel you forward further and faster.

Now, here's something that is a little off the beaten path, another nugget of gold for the person who is setting the pace for business success. Apropos of timing, if your boss is not a morning person, you don't want to be waiting at his or her door when the boss arrives in the morning. If you know the boss is a family person who wants to get home quickly at the end of the workday, you don't show up at the door at 4:15 P.M. with a two-hour project.

So, where's the nugget of gold? Here we go: If your boss likes to look good, and you have something that would make him or her look good, then you tell the boss about it in advance. You don't share it in front of a group because then it's hard for the boss to claim part of the credit. So again, timing is important.

So many people are concerned about not receiving credit for their efforts and they anticipate that the boss will ease them out and take all the bows. WRONG! I don't know that a boss can survive and thrive by your efforts and not be found out in the long run. And, whatever you tell him or her today, you're going to be smarter tomorrow because you're going to know something else the boss doesn't know. You're constantly learning. So my philosophy was and is: *I don't mind sharing what I know with people because they would have to keep up with me every day and I'm going to know something else tomorrow.*

If you introduce something that's new in the presence of the boss and others and it's the first time they're hearing it, many bosses would be offended. That's not because they don't get the credit but because they are surprised and don't appear to be up to speed on what it is that you're doing or have done. So keeping the boss in the loop prevents the boss from getting embarrassed. Sometimes the boss may steal your thunder. But in the long run, most bosses, even if they steal your thunder, are looking out for your career. It's a win-win relationship. You've helped the boss look good; the boss is going to make sure you look good.

Timing is at work in small business settings, too. If you visit your clients on a regular basis, you may know when they're contemplating an expansion, changing to a new system, or adding a new service. If their decisions offer you a business opportunity, and you know that these clients are having a decision-making meeting on Wednesday, you might want to pay a visit on Wednesday. You might be able to answer questions for them. You demonstrate an interest. You get the contract!

6

BEYOND THE STAGE

STEP 7:
Build A Reputation For Good Character

People will judge you by what you do, not what you say. Being trustworthy and having integrity and high moral standards will attract people to you and open doors that might otherwise be shut.

I believe character is about making good choices, being trustworthy, and having integrity and high moral standards. It partners with accountability, accepting responsibility for the choices that you make, good or bad.

When people define your character, they typically focus on what you do rather than what you say or tell them you believe. In other words, your actions speak for you. Good character requires that you "do the right thing," even when it's costly or risky to follow through on a choice you've made. What is the right thing? The answer to this question is not a simple one. Great minds have pondered it throughout the ages. For our purposes, however, let's acknowledge that people tend to determine what the right thing is based upon their personal code of ethics.

A code of ethics can be simply defined as adhering to the Golden Rule, which is generally expressed as "Do unto others as you would have them do unto you." It can be defined more specifically by breaking it out to apply to your personal conduct with friends, family, and colleagues, with examples such as treating all people with respect, being charitable, and showing compassion. Your actions let people know what code of ethics you have adopted. If you know that you will do nothing short of treating all people with respect, for example, then no matter what circumstances arise, you stick to your rule.

Illustration: When I was a third-year student at Tuskegee University, someone who represented a major company interviewed me and other students for jobs. He insisted that students from Tuskegee were not as capable as those attending major universities like the University of Michigan. I disagreed. I enrolled at the University of Michigan for one semester in my senior year and earned grades that proved the interviewer was wrong! I never contacted the man to tell him about my University of Michigan grades but I proved to myself that Tuskegee and I were both doing an admirable job!

You might think my response to his negative assertions was dramatic. It certainly tells you something about my character. *Danny takes it seriously when you challenge his ability to be as good or better than the next guy. He'll go the distance to prove his point. I hope you'll conclude, Danny sets high standards for performance excellence and I want to work with him!*

Illustration: The phrase I heard most often about Americans from people in other countries is . . . "Americans are arrogant." Listening, learning, willing to be humble, and acknowledging that you don't understand work wonders. When I made my first international trip to Costa Rica, we went out to dinner and I assumed, just by observation, that the people at the table were Spanish-speaking. When I sat down and tried my two words of Spanish on them, I realized they didn't speak Spanish and perhaps were expecting me to speak either English or Portuguese, and I wasn't speaking either.

Liana, the lady seated next to me, spoke English and introduced me to everyone at the table and explained to me that they were from Brazil and spoke Portuguese. They understood that I couldn't speak Portuguese and they were going to speak English as best they could so that we could converse. I chose to participate in the conversation and chose to attempt to do the dance they did following the dinner.

The next day, when I gave my speech (with the aid of a translator), the first thing I did was to thank Liana for recognizing that I didn't know what I was doing! I made reference to their dance and the fact that I had a lot to learn about their culture and that I was willing to learn. I didn't come in pretending to be a person who knows everything. I was very humble, and I believe they appreciated it. People can tell if you're interested, caring, thoughtful, and respectful of them. I found that to be true in my travels around the globe.

Think About It

Some people examine a choice they're considering by asking a series of questions. In the book *The Power of Ethical Management* (William Morrow, 1988), the authors, Norman Vincent Peale and Kenneth H. Blanchard, mention these questions:

(1) Is it legal?
(2) Is it balanced?
(3) How will it make me feel about myself?

In business, maintaining good character helps you in your interactions with other people whether you're leading them or working with them on a team or whether you're seeking advice and counsel or giving advice and counsel.

So you either help or hurt your team, depending upon your ability to influence and work with others.

Money Management

A person's approach to money management speaks volumes about character issues. If creditors are calling someone at work, that has to be a distraction. If that someone is sitting at her desk worrying about how she's going to pay her bills, it may lead to credit card abuse and if she has been issued a company credit card . . . well, things can go from bad to worse.

Abuse of the company credit card is not an infrequent occurrence. I think maybe deep down there's the thought, "I'll pay it back when things get better." And then things never get better.

If the company advances you a large sum of money to relocate your family and the money is not managed well and you haven't completed your relocation, that could be a problem. If it's company policy to advance you money to pay closing expenses on your new home or to replace draperies or things of that nature or to pay your hotel and living expenses, you might get a check that would cover two months of living expenses up front. If you take that money and decide that you'd like to have a nice new car, you'd like to go to Las Vegas, you'd like to pay off some of your bills or whatever you choose, then you're not able to complete your relocation.

Lack Of Discretion

I've had to put memos in personnel files a number of times having to do with lack of discretion in handling money. It's not always because a person has financial difficulties at home. There are some people who will manage their money very well at home but they will spend the company's money like it's falling from the trees. I'm not sure what motivates people to do those things, but they do happen, and sometimes you never figure out why they did it.

I've had cases where a manager would go on an international trip and not mention that he was taking his wife, but I found out from one of the secretaries. I didn't inquire about it, but secretaries know it's not right and they'll just say, "Do you know that he took his wife?" It's true that the cost of the room doesn't change, but the food tab increases and the length of the trip is often extended.

So Much Money

I had very little money in college. When I received my first job after college and my first salary, it seemed like so much money. I didn't think of tax implications. I didn't think in terms of net salary. I was thinking in terms of gross salary.

Illustration: I purchased a new car three weeks before my graduation. Rose and I rented an apartment that was probably too expensive for us. Naturally, we wanted to furnish it and we purchased furniture with a credit card. My new job required that I have a new wardrobe. Again, I used the credit card. I should have been saving money and not borrowing and paying a lot of interest. Yes, I heard people say that you should save, but I was waiting for the day when there was money left to save and steadily increasing the amount of money that was being spent. About two years into my career, we were $11,000 in debt, and my salary was $9,000 a year. One day a creditor called me at work and that did it. I took a poster board and listed all of the creditors down the left side. Next to each creditor, I listed the balance we owed. I said, "I'm going to get rid of these balances in 18 months." I divided by 18 and wrote down how much I was going to pay each one each month. We were going to live on what remained and it was very, very small.

As part of the recovery, we moved from a two-bedroom

apartment into a one-bedroom apartment. We didn't have
to do that but I wanted to make this plan work and that was
a way of helping to make it work. I took lunch to work and
we didn't make any trips. We didn't entertain. We basically
shut down for 18 months because there was no greater priority than getting out of debt.

I developed some financial discipline in the process and
a greater appreciation for money, saving money, thinking in
terms of net worth as opposed to income.

For me, the key to managing finances is to get ahead of
the curve so you have money that is invested and is growing
and making money for you. Other people are using your
money and paying you interest rather than you borrowing
money and paying them interest. And to get from one side
of the curve to the other side of the curve, you don't have to
be in a particular income level. You could make the formula
work at almost any income level. But you have to work the
formula. *Plan the work and work the plan.*

Considerable Distraction

Sometimes making a job change, accepting a relocation,
or making some other career-enhancing move is not done
because of all the attention that is focused on the debt problem. Being in debt limits your freedom. It causes a person to
become wed to a single company. And you should strive to
create independence through your financial stability in order to open up options. You won't necessarily exercise them,
but they're available to you.

Let me digress for just a moment. If you are currently
in debt, it's my opinion that the sooner you get out of it, the
better it will be for you as you set the pace for your business
success. I could have tried to get a consolidation loan and
hoped for better times ahead. That is not a good move, and I
bring it into the discussion now just in case you're considering it.

Getting a consolidation loan is like being in the ditch and having someone give you an extra shovel. You run the risk that you are going to start spending over again because suddenly there's money available that was not available before. You could fool yourself into thinking you're now on safe ground because you have a little extra money each month. But that money is really money that you owe, it has simply been deferred because of the consolidation loan. In general a consolidation loan is something to be avoided. If you consider it, it should only be in conjunction with strong financial discipline.

One of the main problems with getting into debt and telling yourself: "Things will change; I'll earn more next year; I'll have consumer credit counselors negotiate with my creditors; I'll borrow from my parents and pay them back very slowly (after all, one day that money will be mine anyway)" is that you're distancing yourself from taking responsibility for your money problems. You are running counter to Step 7 (Build A Reputation For Good Character) *and all that goes with it!*

Accountability As A Measurement Tool

I rely upon accountability as a clear, clean measurement and guideline that keeps me on track. I know I must accept responsibility for the choices I make, good or bad. One of the things I learned about in mid-career was that if you only deliver what is asked for, you don't meet the ultimate requirement. Accordingly, hold yourself accountable to exceed expectations.

The expectation of the person who counts on you is that you will take the requirement and you will enhance it and will come back with something that's even better and greater than what was asked for. Sometimes the person who counts on you doesn't have the time to specify everything. Sometimes a key person knows if he or she drops a hint as to what's necessary, you have the knowledge and the tools (e.g., staff, time, budget) and can come back with things that are even greater than he or she could envision at the onset. An awareness that if you deliver only what was asked for, you haven't met the ultimate requirement is powerful information. Use it.

When anyone is asked to describe your character (e.g., attributes, traits, or abilities) let it be said of you that you are *always willing to go the extra mile. I couldn't ask for more. I hope that a listener will decide, "We gotta have this person come to work with us!"*

STEP 8:
Keep A Positive Attitude

A positive attitude helps you to stay focused on the future and to believe in positive outcomes. You attract others with a positive attitude. You will learn to forgive others and to get over setbacks.

In Viktor E. Frankl's 1959 book, *Man's Search for Meaning*, he writes, "We who lived in concentration camps can remember the men who walked through the huts comforting others, giving away their last piece of bread. They may have been few in number, but they offer sufficient proof that everything can be taken from a man but one thing: the last of the human freedoms — to choose one's attitude in any given set of circumstances, to choose one's own way."

When you wake up in the morning, you can choose the tone of your day by your outlook. Even when you're surrounded by people who don't help to buoy you, you're in charge of your own attitude and that's worthy of note! To me, attitude is a predisposition about a situation, a person, a place. By choosing a positive outlook, you're going to seek out opportunity. You believe a positive outcome is possible. You've allowed yourself to think in those terms, so you're looking for those opportunities.

People reflect back to you what's written on your face. I've tested it! If you go into work and you pump yourself up before you walk into the building and have a smile on your face and a pleasant thought on your mind, *it* (i.e., good vibrations) leaps back at you from those around you. All you've done is made a conscious decision to think positively. It's a wonderful habit to cultivate. If you allow yourself to come in dragging and think about all the things that could go wrong, it can become a habit, too. And if you allow yourself to only hang around with people who do the same thing, it can become ingrained.

Attitude I. Q.

Where do you fit on the Attitude I. Q. (Investigation Quiz)? This short, fun-to-take quiz is designed to alert you to more than one way to assess a situation. Be aware that your choice of words often reveals your attitude.

1. An 8-ounce glass contains 4 ounces of water. Will you report that it's half full or half empty?
   (This is too easy!) Nevertheless, your half-full observation earns you 5 points.
2. Do you refer to a problem or challenge as a problem or a challenge?
   Give yourself 5 points if you think in terms of challenges. That's because a challenge is a dare. A dare suggests that a response shall be forthcoming. You are determined to try to remedy a situation. A problem, on the other hand, doesn't hint at forthcoming action. You may or may not try to improve the situation.
3. The company picnic is rained out. You announce to your staff that the picnic is cancelled. "The wasted picnic food will be available to anyone who wants it at lunch time in the company cafeteria." Or, you announce to your staff, "The company picnic will be held indoors. A complimentary lunch will be served in the company cafeteria."

I leave it to you to decide which one is the positive response that earns 5 points!

4. Marie and Tom hear it on the grapevine. "Company lay-offs are coming at the top of the month." Marie updates her resume and waits. Tom worries and waits.

   Favor Marie's response and earn 5 points. It may be a worrisome time but positive action earns points on the Attitude I.Q.!

5. A job candidate is asked to write a feature article about the company she wants to work for, even though she brings a portfolio filled with her published articles to the interview. Later, she tells a friend that she thinks it's a good way for the company to find the best person for the job. Her friend observes that being asked to write a feature article for the company publication is excessive. She should get paid for her article since she is a professional writer. Her friend adds, "This company may not be the kind of company you want to work for if they take advantage of people."

   Give yourself 5 points no matter which position you take. Each one demonstrates a positive attitude. The friend's characterization of the company may be accurate and her recommendation may provoke the job hunter to get more information and ultimately make a good choice.

Score: If you earned at least 5 points, that's good! If you earned 25 points, that's even better.

Illustration: When I relocated to New Jersey, it was the first time I was separated from my family for weeks and months and I was hurting. And, while I didn't allow the bad attitude to affect my job, it was affecting me personally. I came face to face with the reality that we'd buy half the home for twice the money needed to buy a home in Georgia. I had to get over it. Later, I estimated my poor attitude probably extended my relocation adjustment by 60 days. I should have looked at the move from a different perspective. If what mattered was reaching the long-term goal, and if this particular move, relocation, or job was consistent with getting there, I should have viewed the move as only a distraction. I'd never let a distraction keep me out of the game.

Illustration: This longer illustration spotlights various attributes. From my perspective, it's a story about adversity and silver linings. I've placed it here because, throughout this period, it was especially necessary for me to maintain a positive attitude and keep trying. You'll see how this event reaches far beyond demonstrating how a positive attitude can sustain you in times of trouble. As you read, think about each individual's character traits, too. There's another vital issue at play, too. I disappointed people and that hurt. *Make no mistake about it, when I say this is a story about adversity, I refer to adversity on many levels.*

Once, late in my career, I received a phone call from a vice president who had a job vacancy. He was a division head and was interested in hiring a new chief financial officer. I'm not sure how he got my name, but I was interviewed and offered the job. I conferred with my sponsors, key company people who had advised me in the past, and each one discouraged me from accepting this position. I never ran from difficult assignments before and I thought I could make a positive difference here, so I accepted the job.

When I arrived, I found that the unit was expected to turn a profit at the end of the calendar year, but it was already eight months into the year and the unit was running at a significant loss. What I didn't know was that leadership wasn't necessarily committed to fixing the division's problems and to some extent was in denial. My questions to the controller and others about what was going to happen in the last four months to turn things around were met with smiles and chuckles. At this point, I knew I was in a difficult position but I was determined to make progress. I told my immediate leader that after 30 days on the job, I thought that we were in trouble and I had serious doubts as to whether or not we would make the profit number for the year. I was told not to worry, we always make it up. Two months later, I was positive that we weren't going to hit that number. As a matter of fact, at 90 days on the job, things were worse than before. I contacted my leader, who was traveling at the time, and informed him that I was con-vinced we were going to miss the target number by a sig-nificant amount. He said we'd talk when he returned and he felt there was still a possibility we'd succeed. We did not tell upper management until the 15th of November that we weren't going to make the number. We were asked, "Do you understand what happened?" The answer was, "We understand what happened and what happened was an ab-erration." We scrambled just to make sure the number didn't get worse between the 15th and the end of the year.

We were called back in the spring of the new year when it was evident that problems had not abated. My leader and two of my peers took the position that we're going to make the target number. I was not allowed to contribute at this meeting.

On July 10th, another meeting was called at our boss's office. My peers who were making the promises weren't asked to attend. I had to attend with my boss and was *allowed* to be the presenter. A thirty-slide presentation had been prepared to illustrate the situation. By the time I got to the third slide transparency, the senior vice president reached over, flipped to the last one, and saw that we were admitting to a $50-million-dollar problem. He slammed his hand on the table, walked out of his office, and didn't return. My leader actu-ally asked, "Do you think he's mad?" Obviously, he didn't get it!

I wasn't having the impact I wanted to have. I consulted with a number of people about what to do: try to get out or stick with it? Before I could act, there was a change in lead-

widely known. Many are not well known. You have only to think of the heroes and heroines from literature and from life who inspire you. It may be a family friend or a co-worker who displays this enviable quality. I've selected a few people who are on *Time Magazine's* 100 List (published early in the year 2000). It's a list of 20 people who "articulate the longing of the last 100 years, exemplifying courage, selflessness, exuberance, superhuman ability and amazing grace."

How high do you think each one would rate if there were such a thing as a resilience meter? Probably off the charts! (Note: Learn more about these people via www.time.com. 100 Heroes & Icons.)

Jackie Robinson. Jackie Robinson thrilled sports fans with his performance on the baseball field but that was only part of his story. Jackie shattered baseball's color barrier. If you don't know his story, I recommend you read about him and his years with the Brooklyn Dodgers.

He had to be bigger than the Brooklyn teammates who got up a petition to keep him off the ball club, bigger than the pitchers who threw at him or the base runners who dug their spikes into his shin, bigger than the bench jockeys who hollered for him to carry their bags and shine their shoes, bigger than the so-called fans who mocked him with mops on their heads and wrote him death threats. . . . When Branch Rickey first met with Jackie about joining the Dodgers, he told him that for three years, he would have to turn the other cheek and silently suffer all the vile things that would come his way. . . . When Rickey read to him from "The Life of Christ" Jackie understood the wisdom and the necessity of forbearance.

Helen Keller. Ms. Keller altered our perception of the disabled and re-mapped the boundaries of sight and sense. She was left both blind and deaf by illness before the age of two. She went on to read, write, and speak and became an inspiration to countless people around the globe. Contact the National Women's Hall of Fame or view the *The Miracle Worker*, which was first televised in 1959 and was also adapted for stage and screen, to learn more. It is the story of Ms. Keller and her famed tutor, Anne Sullivan.

Rosa Parks. Her refusal to go to the back of the bus in Montgomery, Alabama, on December 1, 1955, precipitated the bus boycott led by Martin Luther King, Jr. In 1956, the boycott ended after the U. S. Supreme Court ruled bus segregation unconstitutional. Ms. Parks said, "I did not get on the bus to get arrested. I got on the bus to go home." You may want to read more about Ms. Parks, who received the Congressional Gold Medal in 1999. (For more information, see *Time* and www.womenswire.com.)

Jimmy King. Dean, School of Business, Tuskegee University, 1968. Most readers won't know Jimmy King, but he's a hero to me. I had an "A" average and didn't study for the final exam. I thought I could "wing" it. I received a grade of 62, and he wrote across the top of my paper "SHAME ON YOU." I went to his office to see if I could negotiate an "A" and he said, "No way. I know you didn't study." He taught me that when you blow it, you blow it, and you have to accept the consequences.

Howard Carter. Dean, School of Liberal Arts, Tuskegee University, 1970. Carter's comment, "That's their problem. That's not your problem," acted on me like a shot of caffeine at a time when my resilience was down for the count. He said this about folks who make inaccurate statements about the South or fall prey to stereotypes and don't bother to look at facts. "That's their problem. That's not your problem!" This imposing gentleman has my admiration for many of his other virtues, too. But he put things into perspective for me at a critical time during my college days and zing — I was off and running again.

Hercules. Hercules was a mythical Greek hero noted for his physical strength. He faced and defeated countless enemies. Stories of Hercules attest to his courage and resilience. Many latter-day heroes in fiction were crafted in his image. Greek and Roman mythology is rife with such people.

Lillian Fishburne. Rear Admiral. I did not know of her but located her name under "Real African American Heroes." (see: www.raaheroes.com). Among the many awards she has received are the Legion of Merit, the Meritorious Service Medal, the Navy Commendation Medal, and the Navy Achievement Medal. In February 1998, she was promoted to Director, Information Transfer Division for the Space, Information Warfare, Command and Control Directorate, Chief of Naval Operations, Washington. D.C.

Lloyd Ward. In the August 9, 1999, issue of *Business Week*, an article, "His remarkable journey to become Maytag's CEO: The Saga of Lloyd Ward," tells you who he is and where he started from. "The journey began on a narrow country road in southern Michigan. There, in a 20-foot-by-20-foot house with no running water, lived the Ward family." If you're looking for a man of resilience, Lloyd Ward fits the description!

I can't bring this topic to a close without mentioning:

Martin Luther King, Jr. When I was 15 years old, I heard King speak at a church in Selma, Alabama. That was in the mid-1960s. Listeners were transfixed, and I knew I was witnessing greatness.

Andy Young. I think of him as Andy, in spite of the many distinguished positions he has held, including ambassador. I heard him speak at fall fairs, receptions, and on other occasions right here at home in Atlanta.

William J. Clinton. I remember reading an article about Bill Clinton when he was still Governor of Arkansas. Based on that one article, I felt as though I could like this man. I felt he could become President of the United States of America. (The rest, as they say, is history!)

If you need examples of people who are resilient, you don't have to look very far. You do have to remember, however, it is an attribute you must cultivate as you maximize your potential to get what you want. *Now that you believe in positive outcomes, know how to deal with difficult people, prioritize with ease, and have numerous success attributes nailed, you'd be hard pressed to be anything but resilient!*

7

COMMAND PERFORMANCES

Ever notice how in the movies when the villain is chasing the damsel in distress, the music builds to a crescendo? Well, here's the part of *Setting the Pace for Business Success* that provides you with a little background music. Until now, you've been presented with what-it-is and how-to-do-it data. Read the following challenge scenarios and simply tune in to the rhythm and flow of success strategies in action. (Don't miss reading the challenge scenario that introduces music!)

Challenge: Calling the shots when the bad news is gory

At one point, the decision was made to have everyone companywide install and use a new electronic general ledger system. When it was our turn to make the conversion, the systems people and programmers asked to meet with me and my staff.

We met in mid-December and they said, "The good news is we think we can pull off the conversion. The bad news is that it may get bloody." We talked for a while to clarify what they meant. Apparently, they hadn't done all the testing they wanted to do and anticipated finding bugs in the system. I asked, "Can you guarantee me that the blood won't get deeper than knee deep?"

They said they could. I said, "Okay, let's go with it." I didn't know whether the new system would be operative by the first of the month, at the end of the month, or on the 15th of the following month. I envisioned there would be considerable trouble-shooting required but reasoned the reward was worth the risk.

End of January and still waiting

We weren't able to produce any financial reports at the end of January. We did get core information to pass along to the corporate office, but the traditional data that people expected after Christmas wasn't — it just wasn't!

I told people that we'd have results at the end of February and I'd show both months. We'd be able to compare and go from there. I calculated that since we used an annual reporting system, the month of January was the safest month for us to operate without the availability of precise figures. In the end, the new system was operative and there proved to be "much ado about nothing."

Challenge: My boss hurls accusations at me in front of my colleagues.

During a staff meeting with my peers and our boss, our boss accused me of giving inventory statistics to the corporate office without reviewing them with him in advance. His tone was angry, and the charge was unexpected. My response was, "I did not personally release numbers, but it's possible that someone on my staff released numbers. I'm not aware of it, but I will check it out, and I'll let you know what I find out."

Stay calm. Get the facts. Keep the emotion out of it. I rely upon appropriate body language (e.g., people tell me I have a poker face) to come to my aid.

Challenge: A bribe is offered when I've been on the job for one hour!

On my very first day on the job, or should I say night on the job since I was the night manager at a manufacturing facility, within that first hour, there was a train accident at the back of the facility. I was called on my radio and went out to investigate.

As soon as I arrived, the conductor explained to me that he had broken a switch and if it was reported, he would lose his job. He wanted to know if he could pay me to repair the switch and not report the incident. All of my assistants scattered and left me standing there, alone! I said to him, "I don't know what I'm supposed to do, but I do know that I'm not supposed to take money. So I will go back to my office and make some phone calls and I will get back to you." I went back and made phone calls and, apparently, he'd made some phone calls, too. Before I called him back, he called me and apologized for having put me on the spot. We reported the incident and how that affected him I truly do not know.

Challenge: The very first person I had to dismiss was a recent college graduate.

She had attended a major college and earned a very high grade point average, and she was working at an entry-level job. She could not do the job. After about six months of coaching, counseling, documentation, and consultation with human resources and my leader, we concluded that it wasn't going to work out.

I had already informed her that dismissal was a possibility if things did not change. When it was time to deliver the actual message, we went to a private conference room away from the work area. We reviewed everything that had happened throughout that six-month period. One of her questions to me was, "Do you really think I'm that bad or do you think I'm in the wrong profession?" My response was, "I know that you went to a good university and had good grades. What I don't know is why you were unable to do the work. But if your inability to do the work is representative of how you would approach the next job, it may be something to consider. I don't believe that level of performance will sustain you in this profession. And that's my honest opinion."

I really wanted her employment to work out, but at the same time, I prepared the "paper trail" or documentation in case it didn't.

Terminations and demotions are part of the package when you're a leader. Still, what I said was both fact-based and from the heart.

Challenge: I'm the junior person but I've got to tell a senior executive that he's responsible for what transpired.

The call came on a Friday afternoon. Fly to New Jersey to meet with a senior vice president to explain a $27 million expense variance. The main cause of the variance was the addition of people to the payroll to solve a service problem. These additions were authorized by the very senior vice president that my boss and I were going to visit.

How should I tell him that the variance was a result of a decision he made, discuss what we were going to do about it, and manage to exit the meeting room alive? It was clear to me that my intermediate leaders didn't plan to say much.

My strategy was *to say only what was necessary.* I reminded the senior vice president of the meeting in which the additions to the payroll were authorized and quantified the impact those additions had on the main portion of the variance.

I didn't say it was a bad decision. I just identified it as a fact. First, he complimented me on being straightforward and to the point. He said, "Now I understand how it came about. What are you going to do about it?"

I looked across the table to see if I was going to get any assistance and I got blank stares. The message was, "It's up to you. Whatever you say, that's where we're going."

I said, "It seems obvious to me we have to reduce the headcount." He asked, "When are you going to do that?" I said, "The earliest would be 60 days from now." He asked, "Would you do it all at once?" I responded, "No, we'll do it in phases."

The thing that got us through the meeting was the fact that it was focused. It was simple. There was an explanation of cause and effect. I stayed calm. There was an action plan to recover from the problem.

Note: Are you wondering how the solution impacted customer service? Well, this happens a lot in Corporate America — what's hot today may be something different tomorrow. Service had been hot earlier. Budget overrun was hot now.

Challenge: Turning down two promotions and hearing the "Big Boss" say, "Two strikes, and you only get three."

The first promotion I turned down came along when I was working at my first job with the company. It was totally out of finance, and I was committed to finance. Even though there was an increase in salary, I didn't see how that would fit into my long-term strategy. When asked by the manager if I understood that it was a promotion and that there was more pay involved, I said "yes" and explained that it was out of sync with my long-term strategy. I was willing to sacrifice that $60 a month to stay on track.

There was one situation where I was offered a promotion and the offer "went away." (That can happen, too.) I'd already been told about my new salary and basically was waiting for the effective start date. It went away because the person who had to approve it was two levels above, and he didn't think I was ready for the job. Frankly, I wasn't sure I was ready. I had been promoted to supervisor one year earlier and supervised a staff of seventeen people in cost accounting. So when the offer came along, I was still fine-tuning my performance in that job. (I eventually got promoted to the job I'd been denied. Ah, but that's another story.)

The next offer came within five weeks or so of the first offer. The job was in product management. I turned it down. The director called me in and said, "Strike two, and you only get three. I gather you don't want me to ask you again?"

I said, "Only if it's something that is consistent with my aspirations," and he invited me to elaborate. So I gave him an idea of a couple of jobs that I wouldn't mind having. I wouldn't mind having this job, one in New Jersey, and one in Atlanta. When I returned and told my immediate boss that I'd said "no," he said, "No, you didn't." But of course, I did. Less than two months later, I was called upstairs again and promoted into one of those jobs I had mentioned.

It's worth digressing briefly to let you know that you really can stay focused, think fast, and assess the probable ramifications of what's about to come out of your mouth. If you're not yet doing this, recognize that you can and shall do it.

- First, don't get rattled.
- Then, if you know yourself and know your limitations, you'll know if what you've been told to do or encouraged to do is going to fit. You'll know it as soon as you hear it!
- Study other people. As someone builds up his or her case, you know exactly where the person is going and you're there before the individual arrives. You'll have a few moments to figure out how you're going to respond. If you think this runs counter to the

advice people give you to "assume nothing," let me explain. If you see a car headed in a particular direction, you don't have to know where it's going. All you have to do is know the driver, and you know where it's going to end up. You can be wrong! But when you're really good at this, you're listening both to what is being said and what is not being said.

When I returned to the director's office, he didn't ask me. He told me. "We're sending you to Alpharetta, Georgia, to be the new division manager of the operation." And I'd already said I wouldn't mind having that job, so how could I say no?

Challenge: Green circle dilemma and management pals don't want to keep their commitment. I move without them.

In an effort to save money, management shifted employee pay grades. At the time, some employees were already earning wages in excess of the new top numbers. These people were promised verbally, and later in writing, that their wages would not be reduced. Employees whose income was protected were said to be in the "green circle."

I had recently been promoted into the organization. Someone came to me and asked if I'd heard of the "green circle" issue. I asked for an explanation. The employee explained what had happened and why and added that while this was going on, the group had unionized. He wanted to be sure this pay protection was written into the new contract.

I promised to research the issue and, if I could confirm his information, I'd call those at the bargaining table to remind them of the "green circle" pledge. To make a long story short, although this was a bona fide pledge, it was being tossed aside. Some 200 people were going to lose anywhere from $300 - $500 a month. If a husband and wife were both working, it was possible for a family to lose as much as $1,000 a month. I was urged to let it die.

Somebody wrote the chairman of the board and, all of a sudden, everybody was interested. I did another investigation and wrote a two-page white paper to describe the situation. I sent it through channels, and there were phone calls back and forth. Finally, late one afternoon, my leader told me, "We discussed it. We don't think you should pursue this issue. If you decide to do so, the responsibility is all yours."

I asked if my leader was sure about that plan because I knew that I didn't want to be around for the fall-out if we didn't keep our word. When I asked about the rationale for letting it die, I was told it was because these people had organized. But I saw the "green circle" issue as a matter of integrity, caring about those people, and keeping our word. I pursued it. I had to involve a number of other people, including union members. The bottom line was that pay protection was worked into the contract and these people didn't lose their pay.

I got twenty-five letters thanking me for my efforts on their behalf. Guess what? Everybody up the line wanted to know why they didn't get any letters. It reinforced my awareness that everybody wants to be associated with a winning situation! As a matter of fact, there never was a time that I was promoted when fifteen people didn't show up to tell me the role they played in getting me the promotion.

Note: You might be thinking that the other top management people who were prepared to renege on "green circle" issues weren't demonstrating attributes associated with career success (e.g., commitment). Yet these people are in "lofty" places in the organization. I recognize that some people move along with the aggressive do-or-die, run-them-over, just-get-the-result, it-doesn't-matter-what-you-leave-in-between approach.

I was asked in an exit interview just before I retired,

"How do you want to be remembered by those who know you?" I said, "I would like to be remembered as a guy who proved that you can be a nice, regular guy and still be successful." My approach comes complete with a bonus, which is personal satisfaction and peace of mind.

Challenge: Five times when I "lost it"

Budget proposals came in at over 25 percent higher than the year before, and I "lost it." A so-called practical joker wrote an article that could reach 1,500 people in our organization to say I was being transferred from Georgia to New Jersey and I "lost it." These are two of the five times that I "lost it" in my entire career.

We had been given guidelines to hold the budget flat: "Don't raise the budget." I was in Washington, D.C., working on national bargaining issues with the union while my staff was reworking budgets. The budget submission process is a major undertaking, and people go through a lot of steps before each area budget can be compiled into a single budget. When the budget came to my desk, it was 25 percent higher than the year before and I "lost it." Now, 5 to 10 percent over last year's budget wasn't what I wanted either but 25 percent higher was outrageous, and the staff should have known it.

I've thought about the act of "losing it," and I realize my intent was not to vent frustration, even though that was part of it. The intent was to express disappointment and emphasize that we had steered away from what we agreed to do. This was unacceptable, and we needed to get the train back on the track as soon as possible.

An employee who wrote articles for the company newsletter wrote an absolutely false article reporting that I was being transferred to New Jersey. I had only been in Atlanta for a little less than a year at the time. He claimed that he intended it as a practical joke and didn't expect it to be circulated. When I learned about it, I wanted to fire the guy on the spot because I thought it was irresponsible. Who knows how many people read or heard about it? Trying to do   rumor control when you have customers to serve — well, "I lost it."

What saved the guy was that it was a Friday afternoon and I had all weekend to think about it. Over the weekend, I managed to regain my composure. On Monday, I was willing to hear the guy out, along with his immediate supervisor and another person who supposedly encouraged him to do it. They claimed to have accidentally left a copy on the copy machine, and someone saw it and made copies and started to distribute it. He denied involvement in the distribution process but I said to him, "It wouldn't have been there to distribute if you didn't generate it." In the end, only a small number of people saw the article and no real harm was done.

I'll tell you about another time that "I lost it." I spent four years in Dallas. I was in that job longer than any of the other jobs I had with the company. At any rate, I had the notion that the local auditor and I should have the same objective: make sure we were doing the books correctly. I didn't see any reason for us to clash. Well, he wrote a one-page audit report, and 90 percent of the page was devoted to what was wrong in the organization.

"Do you really feel this way about the organization?" I asked. He said, "I think the organization is doing really well." I told him, "Anybody reading this would believe things are all screwed up." I suggested he change the report if he didn't feel that way. He claimed it was policy to write it the way he wrote it. I told him if he had the responsibility and flexibility to write it differently, then he should write something that reflected how he felt about the organization. I was finished with the matter.

This took place on a Friday afternoon and, apparently,

he stewed about it all weekend. On Monday morning, he came into my office and threw his audit manual on my desk. He actually tossed it at me and said, "There it is. Read it." I lost it. I came up out of my chair and told him never to come back into my office again. I called his boss. Of course, he had reached his boss first. He said, "I understand you're upset. Do you want me to have him come over and apologize?"

"I'm not looking for an apology. I want you to get him out of the building!"

Note: The guy did apologize and, just to show you how things happen, a couple of years later, he was out of a job. He came looking for work. One of the managers on my team pleaded his case, saying, "We can use his services." And I actually gave him a job. Later, this manager questioned his decision. I told him, "You decided to pursue it. I supported you. I didn't let the past get in the way. So you have to deal with it."

Challenge: I received my first promotion, and two people quit and one woman cried.

She said it was the worst mistake the company ever made. I felt that each of the two who quit threw away opportunities. Each evidently felt he should have been offered the job. As to the woman who cried, she was fond of the person who was there before. My promotion was destroying her little world. I wasn't expecting anyone to roll out the red carpet, but I didn't expect this either. On a number of other occasions, my promotions were greeted by silence. It was obvious that people who normally spoke with me would pass me in the halls or avoid me at lunchtime.

Note: My recommendation is that when one of your peers gets promoted, the first thing you should do is walk up to him or her and say, "Congratulations!" If you're grooming yourself to be the person others are attracted to, you won't do anything less.

By the way, I was promoted into a cost-accounting department in which I'd never worked. I asked myself, how are you supposed to go in there and manage seventeen people? I didn't know anything about the work they did. But what I found was that every single promotion I got with the company was into an area where I'd never worked. After the first or second time, I said to myself, "Well, okay!" At first, I felt inadequate, although I pretended I was comfortable. Then I gained confidence. It's usual to go through that cycle. Every time you take a new job, you slip back to feeling inadequate. It's just a pattern. You learn that, in time, it's going to go away.

Challenge: Cut the payroll by 200 people and do it without layoffs.

In the mid-1980s, I had my first experience with layoffs and saw some awful things happen. Eventually, I oversaw a $110 million budget and had to make a 10 percent reduction. So $11 million had to be cut, and 60 percent of the budget was people-related expense. I asked for six months to get the headcount down. I believed I could find jobs for these folks. It took us about eight months but we found over 200 jobs. We made the adjustment without laying off a single person. A few jobs were outside the company but most of the jobs were within the company.

In 1995, I was faced with a similar challenge. We arranged for 75 people to take early retirement. We relied on the same strategy of buying time and placing people in other jobs. One of the things that happens in a larger organization is that managers at various levels won't release their people to do other jobs. It's especially true when those people are good performers. If people on your team are capable of finding other jobs, that can save someone else from being laid off. My belief was everybody is "releaseable." Wide adoption of this view helped us meet the challenge.

A Musical Major/Minor Kind of Challenge

I introduced this chapter using the words "performance," "rhythm," and "tune." They help me segue into a song— "Sitting on the Dock of the Bay." I had a lot of fun with this song for about 10 years, and I was called upon to sing it at my retirement party. Lest you think otherwise, "all work and no play" is not a piece of my prescription for success. Let me explain. . . .

About 10 years ago, I was meeting with colleagues at a hotel and, after dinner, there was a karaoke machine available. There weren't many people in the audience, so the crowd was encouraging people to go up and volunteer. The people at my table decided we would draw straws and, of course, I ended up winning! I selected a song I thought I had a shot at singing and hoped that maybe they wouldn't have the song available and that would get me off the hook. But they had "Sitting on the Dock of the Bay" by Otis Redding for me and I sang it.

I didn't realize how many people from the company heard me until the next day when cries of "Sing! sing!" were propelled at me from an audience that had assembled to hear me deliver a speech. A special microphone was waiting at the podium and, in a moment, music was playing softly in the auditorium. So I picked up the mike and started singing. I didn't know how far I'd go. I thought I'd just sing one verse but the audience was responding so favorably, I ventured into the second verse. This was the beginning of a whole series of requests over the next eight years. I sang that song with or without a musical accompaniment on numerous occasions. It was played at my retirement party, and one of the last things I did with my co-workers was to sing to them.

Singing was an unexpected vehicle for letting people know that I'm a regular guy. I'm willing to take a risk. I have a sense of humor and like to have fun.

An International Odyssey

It's not surprising that many unusual circumstances arise when you're traveling great distances from home to conduct business. You may not speak the local language. You may be unaware of the finer points related to a culture or a code of conduct (e.g., arriving later than the appointed hour to attend a function). Time, weather, and food differences often demand that you make radical adjustments. Some of my international experiences are scattered throughout this book to illustrate various points. But there's more! As you read, ask yourself what you would have done in the same set of circumstances. This exercise is intended to demonstrate that there are always options. As you consider what your course of action would be, take note of how I fared based upon my choices. Since hindsight is 20/20, I can tell you without hesitation if I had to do it all over again, I would change almost nothing. That's because the success attributes that work for me everywhere else didn't fail me during my international odyssey.

Challenge: I am hospitalized in Mexico City.

I'd had minor surgery but was given the okay by my doctor to travel. I flew to Mexico to attend a meeting, and the evening I arrived, I had dinner with Lucent colleagues who had flown in from other countries. Everything was normal, but when I woke the next morning, I noticed I had started to bleed. I thought the bleeding would stop and went to the meeting. I went to the men's room every hour to see if the bleeding had stopped and I explained my frequent exits by being candid about my situation.

Other heads prevail

At around 11:00 A.M., people approached me and said, "We think we need to call a doctor." I said, "I want to go to the airport and go back to the United States." They advised that I see a doctor without delay and arranged for a doctor to come into the conference room to examine me. His recommendation was that I immediately go to the hospital. They actually brought an ambulance out to the building and put me on a stretcher and took me to the hospital. The English-speaking manager went with me. He told me what the doctors were saying. I told myself, "Don't panic."

Six or seven hours later, I was released from the hospital and returned to the hotel. People who were aware of my situation were waiting for me and presented me with a beautiful gift. I said, "I'd like to join you this evening, but obviously I had better get some rest." I went to bed and the next day flew back to the United States. The English-speaking manager flew with me to make sure I was okay.

I have a tendency to trust people after I know them for a little while. I had been to Mexico City before and knew many of these people for at least a few months. I believed they asked me to go to the hospital because they were genuinely interested in my well-being. When I said I wanted to return home and they asked me to see a doctor immediately, I trusted them and responded accordingly.

What would you do given the same set of circumstances?

(A) Contact your home physician
(B) Travel home immediately
(C) Place your trust in the people around you

Challenge: I use a translator to help deliver my speech, and the wrong language is plugged into my ear.

The very first time I spoke to a group of people with the aid of a translator, I learned about using ear sets. If you put in an earpiece to hear the question and neglect to remove it when you answer the question, you're going to hear Portuguese (or whichever language is being used) conversation in your ear. It's a tad disorienting. I was standing in front of an audience of 100 people and had already experienced a comedy of errors leading up to this speech and now this! I laughed. I took off the earpiece. Everyone else laughed.

After the speech, I told listeners that I had a lot to learn. I told them I didn't speak their language, but I was genuinely interested in knowing about them and their issues, and I wasn't going to change anything until I learned enough to make smart changes. I took some questions from the audience and, at one point, practically got a standing ovation.

What would you do given the same circumstances?

(A) Spend time with translators and ask for tips before I make an appearance
(B) Probably make mistakes
(C) Keep my sense of humor in good working order

Challenge: Deliver satisfaction guaranteed. End of sentence.

A Mexico-City-based client called me to tell me he was dissatisfied with the service one of my managers provided. I told him I'd fly down to discuss his concerns. I had met him once before. When I arrived, he spent about fifteen minutes expressing his displeasure, but he apparently wasn't telling me everything. Soon after I returned to Georgia, he called again. I agreed to return to see him. This time he was ready to detail his concerns. I listened carefully. When he finished speaking, I asked him if I had his permission to invite the manager to join us so that he could hear about the concerns, too.

Together, we were able to identify some specific areas where changes could be made that would satisfy this client. He was very pleased.

What would you do given the same set of circumstances?
(A) Attempt to resolve matters via the telephone and not fly back and forth

(B) Ask for a longer first meeting and ask probing questions
(C) Tell the manager to handle things and keep me advised
(D) Meet with the client as often as necessary

Challenge: No one meets me and *no comprende.*

On one occasion when I arrived at the airport in Mexico City, the Lucent manager who was based there was supposed to pick me up. But after I arrived and went through customs, he wasn't there. I didn't think he missed seeing me because I'm tall and we'd met before. Mexico City is very large, with 10 to 15 million residents, and the airport is a beehive of activity. Since I don't speak the language, I couldn't use the phone efficiently. My best option was to wait and see if he was just running late. He arrived fifteen minutes later and off we went.

What would you do given the same set of circumstances?

(A) Call my home office and let them find out what's going on
(B) Take a taxi (I'd write down the destination address and let the driver read it.)
(C) Tell the manager I was annoyed by his tardiness

Challenge: I'm stranded on an airfield in a remote area.

Waiting to be picked up at an airport in Mexico City is frustrating, but here's an experience that tops it! On my first trip to Costa Rica, I knew the meeting was going to be in a remote area but I didn't know how remote. The first flight landed at a major airport in San José. I was met and escorted to a smaller airport and boarded a plane that could only hold six passengers. The two pilots asked me in broken English if I knew where I was going. I don't speak Spanish but managed to convey that I didn't know. I only knew the name of the hotel. They somehow determined where they thought I was supposed to be going and told me they figured it out.

So we took off and, after flying for about one hour, they brought the plane down. I kept looking for an airport. I didn't see one. I didn't see cars or buildings or anything. We rolled up to the end of a little airstrip in the middle of a field. The only things we saw were horses and cows.

The pilots turned to me, "Is someone meeting you?" I nodded "yes" and told myself, "Don't panic." Some kids came out of nowhere, apparently intrigued by the airplane. The pilots talked to the kids and learned there was a pay phone some distance away. One pilot paid a boy for the use of his bicycle. He bicycled to the distant telephone and called the hotel where I had a reservation. He learned that a driver and limousine had been dispatched to pick me up, but the driver was running late.

I was making this trip to deliver a speech to Lucent employees. From the beginning, I thought some of the travel plans were too vague. At one point, I said to my secretary, "If they can't be any more specific than that, I'm not going."

What would you do given the same set of circumstances?

(A) Not travel unless all connections and arrangements were clear
(B) Question the pilots' motives when they landed in this remote place
(C) Refuse to make this trip again!

Note: When I talk to people who are just getting started in international travel, I tell them, "In every case of the unexpected my rule is d-o-n-'t panic!" In this case, the opportunity to panic was compelling. On the many trips that followed, I always took a few minutes to relax and think about my options. I gave things a chance to unfold if they weren't exactly perfect, and it almost always worked out.

By the way, when I showed up to give the speech, no

one was there. I learned that, in Latin countries, people don't show up at the appointed hour. They always arrive later. Soon afterward, 100 people filed into the room.

Challenge: My flight to Argentina is cancelled. What now?

I was traveling with two people from Brazil to Argentina. We had our tickets, but when we arrived at the airport to catch our early morning flight, we learned it had been cancelled. We looked at each other and, since we couldn't speak Portuguese, we used body language to ask, "What do we do?"

Sometimes, you'll find a person who can speak English well but other times, no one speaks it at all. This time, the ticket agent motioned for us to wait and took our tickets across the way to another counter, where she engaged in conversation with that agent. A few minutes later, she returned with new tickets and pointed the way to the airline gate. We found out that we had first-class tickets to Buenos Aires!

What would you do given the same set of circumstances?

(A) Try not to panic!
(B) Try to learn some key phrases in other languages such as: "What do we do?"
(C) Travel with someone who knows the languages of the areas I must visit

Challenge: I arrive in Costa Rica with the wrong kind of clothing.

For a trip to Costa Rica, I packed clothes suitable for fall weather, but a dramatic change in temperature took place. When I arrived, my colleagues asked for my measurements. Within 30 minutes, they arranged for me to have two or three pairs of slacks and two or three shirts so I could be comfortable. Granted, we worked for the same company, but they took unusual steps on my behalf. I complied with their request and expressed my appreciation.

If virtual strangers asked for personal information, such as your measurements, would you:

(A) Think they were impertinent?
(B) Appreciate their kindness?
(C) Tell them to forget about it?

Challenge: Always plan ahead!

When I was initially assigned responsibility for company operations in China and Singapore, I was given very little notice. I had to learn quickly about the region — the language, the culture, and the best way to get there. Since I speak only English, I chose to fly east so that I could change flights in Europe, where English is generally spoken. I had my secretary arrange for an in-country escort and a translator when the language was different. I also called a friend who lived in the region for some additional tips. I found that planning ahead made these trips much more successful.

If you were about to travel, would you:

(A) Call a travel agent to obtain background information and bypass your secretary?
(B) Ignore the travel-related details and focus on business goals?
(C) Obtain stacks of current information about the destination country and read?

8

WHAT EVERY GOOD LEADER
SHOULD KNOW

T HIS CHAPTER IS comprised of *Twenty-Five Lessons Learned* with, in most cases, an added explanation, observation, or comment. Feel free to scan it from time to time. Just as one successful C.E.O. of my acquaintance has a habit of reviewing names in his Rolodex at the end of each week to remind him if he is neglecting anyone he doesn't want to neglect, you can scan this list to see if you have been neglecting to make use of some valuable information. This is a good time to mention that it doesn't matter if you're male, female, young, old, physically challenged . . . well, you get the idea. The focus is on good leaders. Don't be concerned about being a good female leader or a good young leader. Strive only to be a good leader. To think otherwise doesn't enhance your performance.

1. *When elephants fight, it is the grass that suffers.* This is an anonymous African proverb. It's an excellent way to express that you should always use power wisely. Those who are affected will never forget. It bears (or elephants) remembering.

2. People judge you by how well you keep your commitments. A leader is judged by what he or she does. But long before you achieve leader status, the same holds true.

3. Don't ever assume that no one's watching. Always behave admirably. If others notice, and they often do, you'll be pleased to be found out!

4. Always anticipate questions before you make a presentation. It's a dictum in the legal profession and one you're wise to adapt. You'll have time to consider your responses and avoid being tempted to shoot from the hip. You may even decide to shift the focus of your presentation to avoid raising questions you don't want to answer.

5. If a job is worth doing, it's worth doing correctly. This lesson is repeated early and often to schoolchildren. It's applicable in the classroom and on the way to the boardroom!

6. Be willing to stretch and move beyond your comfort zone. There's nothing wrong with having a comfort zone, but if you're within it all the time, you don't know what you're missing.

7. To be successful, you have to go where the action is — whether it's headquarters or Hollywood. Or to say it another way, you can't help the chef prepare the meal if you're not in the kitchen. In either case, you're better able to satisfy your hunger.

8. Learn to be a good listener and to read nonverbal communication (a.k.a. body language). This is critical in maintaining an excellent working relationship with your boss. You'll soon know how a spy who has broken a communication code feels; extraordinarily well informed.

9. Your first priority on any job is to clearly understand your boss's style and expectations. The second priority is to understand the needs of your clients, and the third is to understand the needs of your team.

10. *You may not enjoy some of the jobs you perform, but you can learn from all of them.* Your positive attitude enhances the value of time spent at these tasks.

11. *Take on difficult assignments.* This will separate you from the pack. Management will notice you. When the topic of advancement is raised, you want to be remembered!

12. *Never shoot from the hip. Do your homework and have a plan.* If you must occasionally circumvent this lesson, your general wealth of information should come to your aid.

13. *Surround yourself with people who can help you achieve your goals.* Why try to reinvent the wheel? Every successful person received help along the way.

14. *Reflection is a powerful way to learn from your experiences.* When you're dancing as fast as you can, you don't have time to reflect. From time to time, stop dancing.

15. *Most decisions simply require gathering the facts and applying common sense.* If it sounds too simple, that's because it is simple.

16. *When you attend a meeting, you're fair game.* Just because your boss or another senior person is sitting next to you, don't assume you'll be shielded. There are times when you'll be out there by your lonesome. Be prepared.

17. *Just because someone says you can't put a bowling ball through a garden hose, it means that nobody has done it yet.* I know that my team and I made incredible things happen. It helps when you can get your team to believe it first!

18. *The job of a leader is to set the direction, establish the priorities, choose the team, and change the players when they don't perform.*

19. *Don't get locked into a linear way of thinking.* The world doesn't work that way. A "deliverable" has to be defined each time you're called upon to produce it.

20. *Don't let "distractions" keep you out of the game.* This happened. That happened. This person perplexes me. That issue won't go away. You won't be able to solve all the world's problems during your lifetime. So get over it!

21. *Character is about what you do when nobody is looking.* People either have good character or they don't. A person of poor character can change if he or she wishes to do so. No one else can do it for the person.

22. *See yourself as capable of doing multiple things.* You increase your value to the organization and to yourself.

23. *You can be the leader and not know what's going on —* *temporarily!*

24. *If you're not a "player," people don't miss you when you're not there.* And if they don't miss you, they're not going to invite you.

25. *Don't criticize a person in front of a group.* When you do criticize, focus on the act rather than the person. It's the quickest way to accomplish the goal. Moreover, it's a decent way to do business!

9

NO ONE KNOWS IT ALL

Someone asked me if I walk into situations where people are intimidated by my success. "When you taught for one year in the School of Business at Tuskegee University, were other professors a little threatened by your achievements in the business world?" The question surprised me. I tried to be a regular professor. I didn't pretend to know something if I didn't know it. We spoke to each other, and many were curious about corporate America.

I wanted to know if the students I gave good grades to were getting good grades in other professors' classes, too. I wanted confirmation that my grading approach was in line with standard practices. Respecting all people, being a person of integrity, doing what you believe is right because you can't do it any other way — these attributes support you over and over again. You don't have to remind yourself that no one knows it all; it's merely understood. Nevertheless, I included a chapter on the topic because there's more than one way to examine the concept, and it gives me the opportunity to share experiences that may surprise you.

A Manager Who Reported To Me Committed Suicide

Co-workers made a request that was difficult to grant. The manager had come to me and asked for time off, explaining that his doctor recommended it. He had about 300 people reporting to him. I told him to take the time off since his health was more important than anything else and not to worry about it. When news of his demise came to us, everyone demanded to know what happened. I had no idea. I reluctantly resolved to call his wife and speak with her. She explained to me that he had been depressed for a long time. He left a suicide note saying, among other things, his act had nothing to do with his job. She also said, "We're not going to have a service because he requested that we not have one."

These words played over and over in my thoughts. Ultimately, I bowed to the wishes of people at work who knew him and wanted to have a service. I felt it would help the grieving process. I remember looking out the window and thinking about this for a long time. What is the right thing to do? I decided not to contact his wife again because I didn't want to put her in a position of having to say yes or no. A church service was scheduled. I was asked to be the speaker. The night before my wife, Rose, asked me what I was going to say. I had no idea.

When I got up to speak, I said, "I know there are a number of people in the audience who would like to be up here to say something about this man. Since I've been asked to speak, I will do my best to speak for all of us when I tell you about my experience with him."

I spoke about how I knew him as a friend and how I knew him as a co-worker. I included how he had helped me tremendously when I first assumed the position I held in this 1,500-person organization. I concluded with, "We will miss him. I hope that everyone is comfortable that I've said something that he or she would have said if given the op-

The demoted employee brought the incident to my attention. I assured her I would get the facts and act accordingly. I checked the records, and she was correct. There was an audible "buzz" in the department when I called the outspoken employee into my office. Before I could introduce the issue, she interrupted me. "I know why you called me in here. Everybody out there is waiting to see what's going to happen. I think you're doing the right thing because I knew a week ago that I should have been the one to be demoted, not the other woman."

She told me that she knew I was a man of integrity and there was no need to spend time talking about the mistake. "Let's talk about something else." We spent about 20 minutes talking about her farm and chickens and things that she was doing outside of work. She finished by telling me that she was usually outspoken because integrity is often lacking. All she wanted was for people to act with integrity, even when it impacted her negatively. Her response surprised me, and I found her approach to be refreshing. I was happy to know she was remaining in the company.

Good Information

No one knows it all. Successful people work to stay well informed. They're willing to learn new things, don't rely solely upon hearsay, and take time to gather facts.

Speaking of which . . . I think your efforts are enhanced when you're in good physical condition (i.e., get sufficient sleep, exercise, appropriate diet), but I'm not an expert on physical well-being. I also know that being dressed and groomed appropriately is important, but I'm not an image expert. A command of business etiquette and other kinds of know-how support you as you strive to become the one who is sought out for advancement. Go where you must to obtain good information about all of these components. (Don't miss the "Worth Reading!" list at the end of the book.)

portunity." I was amazed that people lined up to t
as I left. Many explained, "Now, it will be easier
on." It was then that I saw the wisdom in doing
realized I'd made the right decision.

Working With Someone I Didn't Know To Mal Funeral Arrangements And Look After The Immediate Family

I was given stewardship over the process of ;
the wife of a manager who suffered a sudden, mass
attack and died. He and his family were from anotl
and he'd been in town to attend a meeting. As a n
fact, he and I were supposed to take a trip togetl
Tuesday. He was at the local shopping mall with hi
the Friday before when he was stricken.

AT&T leaders decided to pay expenses beyond t
because the deceased and his family were far from
worked out the logistics with his wife and then flew
sas City to attend the funeral and make sure that if sh
anything, it was handled. Did I know how to proce
really. But I was proud of the way company mana
responded and believe I helped to make a terrible s
just a little more manageable for the man's wife and

The Wrong Person Was Demoted And It Was Necessary To Target The Most Vocal Employee

During a period of downsizing in Dallas, we u
process called "bumping." A long-time employee o
one with an excellent record of performance w
"bumped" into a job rather than laid off. Employees v
least amount of time with the company or the leas
able job performance records would be demoted or l

One person in the accounting department was d
when the most outspoken person in the department
have been demoted. Everyone was waiting to see if, i
to avoid having to deal with her, I would just let it p

SECTION TWO

A TOPNOTCH COACH:
HOW TO FIND ONE — HOW TO BE ONE

In the tradition of exceeding expectations, a philosophy I enthusiastically embrace, I'm adding a small section to this book that you probably didn't expect. You already know that I wrote this book because I want to help others succeed. I want people to know that no matter what adversity they face, real or imagined, it cannot stop them from attaining "lofty" goals. I did. I can show you how. This book delivers on that promise.

The road to business success would be lonely and more difficult if there were not coaches to assist you along the way. The good news is that you don't have to go it alone. You may already have an up-close, in-your-face personal coach and you may not know it. Or you may want to find a coach and you may not know how to do that. All that is about to change.

The Characteristics Of A Great Coach

A person who is a coach enjoys seeing others succeed. It may be that today's coach was successfully coached at an earlier time or that he or she read about the great work that others did in the past to help make the world a better place. It may be that the coach concluded that one of our purposes here is to make the world a better place and coaching is one way to do it. A good coach gives back some of what he or she has learned and knows that coaching completes the circle of success. Accordingly, a great coach doesn't have a hidden agenda.

Beyond this, good coaches come in all sizes and shapes and can be found anywhere. A coach doesn't have to be high on an organizational chart. He or she should be genuinely interested in you and your success.

Add It Up

A great coach will:

- Listen! Take time to understand you and your circumstances.
- Respect your goals.
- Help identify resources that will provide you with needed skills.
- Act as a "sounding board" when you weigh your options before making a decision.
- Challenge you. Push you beyond your comfort zone.
- Not necessarily be the only coach you have. A great coach may be with you for several assignments, several levels of increased responsibility, but at some point, the nature of your challenges or physical location (e.g., working in a different country) could result in one great coach being less able to perform well. That happens if the coach is no longer prepared to challenge you, identify resources, or serve as a well-informed "sounding board."

Illustration: My very first department head was very influential in coaching me and helping me develop skills. He pushed me out of my comfort zone, helped me build self-confidence, and demonstrated that performance that was just good wasn't good enough.

During the long time that I knew him, he moved up one level on the organizational chart. I got the impression that he loved what he was doing so much that unless it was a promotion in the same line of work, which he eventually got, I don't think any other job would have been of interest to him.

The value of keeping the same coach is that you don't have to start over to explain yourself. Nevertheless, if you outgrow a coach you admire and are tempted to go it alone, consider this: when I had a coach, I felt that I was focusing, making progress, and had someone I could turn to if I had questions or concerns. I had TRACTION!

Why Not Rely On A Spouse Or Good Friend To Assist You?

Given that a spouse, friends, and others who know you on a more intimate level might have excellent qualifications for the job, it's impossible for them to be "straight with you." One, they don't want to hurt your feelings. Two, they want to maintain a relationship that's beyond the business of coaching. Three, a decision or direction you consider may have direct impact on them, and they're rendered helpless to be impartial.

The Student Chooses The Teacher

It's difficult for a coach in the business place to choose someone to coach. It's easy for the person who wants a coach to choose the coach. If you've never coached anyone, and you're approached by someone who seeks your counsel, you're obviously the kind of person who attracts people to you. In order for a student/coach relationship to be productive:

- Do you have to like the student?

- What must occur to make you want to take on the job of coach?

The fact is, you may not know very much about the prospective student, but you'll want to work with someone who is accountable and willing to make an effort. And one thing I learned about coaches is if one learns that you're not following his or her advice, the relationship will be short-lived.

Illustration: When I was a relatively new manager working in Dallas, I noticed that Mary, a young woman in the department, had been doing a single job for an extended period of time. I thought she was bright and articulate and had great people skills. Mary really enjoyed what she was doing, but the job was essentially a deadend. I encouraged her to consider a different job, one that would give her more exposure and would allow her to use her people skills and the knowledge she had already acquired. She took the job, did extremely well, and was eventually promoted to a second-level manager position, where she was more influential and had more power.

I didn't wait for her to approach me. I was acting as a coach because I wanted to help and saw an opportunity to help. I was acting as a sponsor because I was trying to build up the pool of talent in my organization.

- I talked to Mary about her interests. Why did you choose the job you held for so long?
- I talked to Mary about her strengths and weaknesses. Do you like working with people? Are you a detail person?
- What do you want to do long term?
- Are you mobile?
- Would you consider a position outside of finance?
- I coached Mary on not losing her cool and on staying calm.

One day, Mary, who observed me coaching other people in the organization, said "I don't understand why you waste your time with those people." I asked her what she meant by "those people." After she explained that she didn't believe they had what it took to be successful, I told her that it's my philosophy that everybody has potential and everybody can be better. If they're on the payroll, I surely hope they're making contributions. And if they're on the payroll, I have an opportunity to coach them and encourage them and give them an opportunity to improve. So I think it is time well spent.

The exchange was eye opening for Mary in terms of rethinking how you relate to people around you, how you judge people, and why it's important to give back and to coach and to develop and to seek the best in everybody.

I coached Mary for about three years. During those years, she returned to me several times and said, "Now I understand what you were talking about."

I mention this to let you know that the coaching experience doesn't immediately impact the student. The coach plants seeds. Eventually, the student experiences "aha!" moments.

At the time I coached Mary, I'd already had a tour at the corporate office, which broadened my perspective. I had worked in a different factory and with different groups of people. In the process, I'd learned a number of things about dealing with people in general. So sharing those things with Mary was beneficial. I found, in many cases, she had to encounter the situation once again and then could look at it differently.

Illustration: (I've had this happen a number of times, so I'll just give you a generic description.) People come to me and say they have issues with their supervisor and they say he's this, that. She's this, that. There are no opportunities. And I ask, "Have you ever asked your boss why? Did you try to get a face-to-face assessment?" Inevitably, the response is, "Well, not exactly."

Make An Appointment

My recommendation is to make an appointment with your boss. Tell the boss you are interested in getting some feedback so you can improve your performance. Take a blank pad of paper with you to use for jotting notes. When the boss speaks, don't say a word. Just listen. And write, even if the boss says something you don't agree with; you want to hear it all. If you interrupt and then you object, that's where the boss is going to stop. You won't ever know what he or she really thinks. It's important to know what the boss thinks, even if you don't agree.

I've had so many people come back and tell me, "When I did that, I found out so many things I didn't know and, you know, the boss isn't so bad after all."

You may be thinking why not wait for your job performance review? Here's why not: it probably happens once a year and may be tied to an increase in salary. If you're troubled by what you hear, the boss is likely to become defensive. In short, it's not a venue for just listening. It doesn't give you the same opportunity to learn what you can do to make a difference.

Tough-Guy Leader

I think it's important to know that sponsors exist! Moreover, sponsors exist regardless of the size of the organization. If there are as many as two people in an organization, one can be a sponsor. They're involved in almost every promotion when a person starts climbing that proverbial ladder of success. Sponsors may vary in terms of their importance to your career, but they're always there and they're always important. You'll be well served when you become the kind of person who attracts sponsors.

The process makes me think of the stock market. Investors place their money in places where they think there will be growth, and sponsors invest in people they believe are going to grow. You have to live up to a sponsor's expectations because, just as people will sell their stock, sponsors will divest their interest in you if performance is disappointing. Sometimes Wall Street surprises investors and investors don't jump the ship. A sponsor may help you figure out to some degree how to get out of a difficult position you're in, but the sponsor is probably only going to do that once.

How I Met The Man Who Was To Become My Long-Term Mentor/Sponsor

I was working in New Jersey when we had a change of leadership. The new vice president had a reputation for no-nonsense operations. "He'll chew you up and spit you out. He'll tell you exactly what's on his mind. If you walk in unprepared — well, just don't!" His reputation preceded him and it's probably why I, who was a junior staff member, was sent to meet with him to review the budget.

I made my presentation very carefully. I only said what I had to say. I learned in that first meeting that he got great joy from finding a single error. I had been so careful to make sure there were no mistakes. But he found one. I could tell by the look on his face that it didn't matter what else I said, he was now happy that he had been able to show me how sharp he was.

It was an important lesson for me. It's effective to understand the person you're talking with and know what motivates the person, what ticks him off, what gets him excited. I went back into his office a number of times, and he always reminded me that he found the one error. Our association led to my being assigned to a new staff and he became the vice president of that staff.

He ultimately sent me to Dallas, where I learned so much. I realized I wasn't wanted there because they viewed me as a spy. Of course, I wasn't! But when he came to Dallas, he would always give me attention that made it obvious that there was some kind of connection. If there were a meeting and an agenda, he made sure I was on that agenda. If I was speaking, I got more airtime. I suspect others reasoned I was sent by the general managers' boss and sooo . . . .

Our relationship led to his becoming my unofficial mentor through most of my career. And since he was so influential and had acted as a mentor to so many others, many of them acted as my mentors. When he found a weak spot, I didn't argue. I listened. I didn't try to weasel out of it or get defensive. I just said, "Yep — you're right."

What's The Difference?

A sponsor does something that's self-serving. That's not a judgment call; it's a fact. A sponsor puts key people into positions where they may help the sponsor look good. A sponsor develops a pool of talent he or she calls upon. In the case of this sponsor, and I had others, people said, "If you worked for him, you gotta be good. If you worked for him and you're still here . . ." and they would laugh!

I Disappointed My Sponsors

It happened when I accepted a position they advised against and it turned out I'd made a major mistake. I knew I was disappointing a lot of people because I was not having the impact I wanted to have.

My sponsors were involved in helping me get back on my feet and into the final job I had with Lucent. I hope they believed that I was a good guy who just happened to get caught up in a bad situation, and I did the best I could, but it just didn't work out.

I think everybody deserves a second chance, but if there's a third or fourth time, it would have to be an extraordinary situation. That's because you hope the person learned from the first experience. Now if it's a different problem, I understand that. As a person grows and learns, he or she will make mistakes.

Understand Why

When I coach people, I tell them to be sure you understand why you made the first mistake because that's one you never want to make again. It's understood that you may make new mistakes.

A coach may try A, B, and C to remedy a situation but it takes two! You don't control the other person's responses or actions. Because you're a person of good character and honor your commitments, you're likely to be tenacious about finding solutions. There are times when you have to let it go! If you don't, you can beat yourself up pretty badly, and there's nothing good to be gained from that drill. Move on.

Giving Back, An Action That Enriches All Concerned

I left my assignment in Dallas in 1988 and returned to New Jersey. I noticed a second-level manager in the systems organization who was very bright. But I also noticed that he allowed people to make jokes about him. He seemed to enjoy it. If he did something dumb, he would come to the office and tell people at higher levels about the dumb thing he did.

I called him aside one day and said, "I know you enjoy the attention that you're getting from these people, my boss, and others. But do you realize those people are discussing you even when you're not around? They're making 'Nelson jokes' and in the long term, I don't think that's good for your career." I told Nelson that he was a talented man with a great future ahead but, "I would not participate in playing little games around the office, like doing things to your computer so that when you come back to it, something strange happens. Those things are not what you want to be known for in the long run."

He took my advice and stopped behaving that way. He came back about two years later and thanked me because, by that time, he was able to reflect on how those things had negatively impacted him. I sponsored him into a key job and everybody thought I was out of my mind for doing this. But I had confidence in him. He came out of a systems position to assume the job I offered him. It was the number one accounting job in my organization. He did well. Later I promoted him to a third-level manager's position. I was the controller for AT&T's largest business unit and I promoted Nelson into the planning job. It involved developing plans — long-range plans, financial plans, budgets — and was dramatically different from his accounting position. He had to deal with numerous complicated issues.

After about eighteen months in the job, he called me and said he needed to talk to me. He was planning to leave the company as early as the following week. We talked about why. He said he just couldn't deal with the situation in New Jersey. I suggested that he view his current situation as a "tour" — not the end of his career. It was a transition. "Of course you want to move, but you came here for learning." He decided to stay with the company but to seek a different assignment. He took a job in London and was very successful. He was promoted twice and he eventually returned to the United States and was promoted again. As I write, he's the chief financial officer of a Silicon Valley company. (Note: You may want to review the letter Nelson wrote about our sponsor relationship, which appears earlier in this book.)

Illustration: One morning, I had breakfast with Jim, who worked in the engineering department. We'd known each other for about ten years. He was expressing disappointment in his lack of career progress. He told me what some of the issues were and said, "I wish I knew someone in engineering that had the level of authority or a position that's comparable to yours. I know you, but you're in finance."

I asked him if he'd consider a position in finance. He laughed and said, "I'll consider anything." About a year later, I had a job vacancy, and I thought of him. I knew he had excellent leadership skills. If you've got great leadership skills, you can learn the technicalities of finance over time.

He also had an MBA. I interviewed him and promoted him into that job. I coached him on how to deal with the people in finance and encouraged him to seek out people who could help him with things he wasn't familiar with and invited him to call me with questions or to discuss difficulties that might arise. He was functioning at a remote location, so I was managing him via the telephone. I had confidence that if he was in the right environment and had the proper coaching, he could make the transition into finance. It wasn't one of our "heavier" financial jobs, and the plan was to put him there and eventually move him closer to the core as he learned more about finance. Jim was successful in the assignment. I moved him to his second assignment, which was totally different. He was successful in that assignment, and he's now vice president of operations for a company on the West Coast.

Jim once said he'd never relocate! Not only did he relocate, he changed careers! He was open to new possibilities, willing to make changes. (He worked on himself, and I was drawn to him. The process plays out every day.) As a matter of fact, he telephoned me recently from an airport in Reno to say "hello" while he was waiting for a connecting flight.

Drawn To Him

I think there's something like a sixth sense that comes into play because you can look at the facts sometimes and you think that this person has great ability and something inside of you keeps saying, "I don't think so." When you're able to look at the facts, you find many people have the same basic credentials. But there's something about the individual that suggests success is hidden within. You sense it. You encourage that person to go beyond where they might otherwise go.

Money Talks

I'll soon travel to Tuskegee, Alabama, to Tuskegee University to sponsor a luncheon for the graduating seniors. Many of them were students of mine when I taught at the university one year ago. I'll thank the faculty of the business school and the graduating seniors for the opportunity they gave me to get to know them, and I'll wish the graduates well, encouraging them to be successful in their careers. I'll also make a financial contribution to the university. I'd be remiss if I wrote about giving back and failed to remind readers about the importance of financial donations.

It's Your Turn

My goal in writing this book was to share some valuable lessons I learned in my twenty-eight-year business career. It is my hope that you have found the nine-step process and the many illustrations compelling. You are now ready to design your own career. You are ready to change the circumstances you have to the circumstances you want.

A percentage of the population will choose to live by design rather than "go with the flow." By choosing a career that you have a passion for and using the tools provided in this book, you will become a person who lives by design. You will set the pace for business success.

Good luck and best wishes on your journey!

Appendices

WORTH READING!

Spend time in bookstores! The areas where I hang out are the business, self-help, and inspirational sections. If a title catches my attention, I look at the contents page and maybe read the foreword or the introduction and try to size up the book. I want something that will enhance what I know or introduce something new. I don't head for a particular author's books because I don't shop by author. I shop by title and content. Here are some books I found to be worthwhile. You may want to read them, but don't stop with these titles because learning is a never-ending process:

Take Time for Your Life by Cheryl Richardson. (1999, Broadway Books)

Take Yourself to the Top by Laura B. Fortgang. (1998, Warner Books)

The Magic of Thinking Big by David J. Schwartz. (1959 - 1965, Prentice-Hall and 1987, Simon & Schuster)

Attitude Is Everything by Keith Harrell. (2000, Harper-Collins)

The Big Picture by Ben Carson. (1999, Zondervan)

The 7 Habits of Highly Effective People by Stephen Covey. (1989, Simon & Schuster)

You Can Make It Happen by Stedman Graham. (1997, Simon & Schuster)

The 21 Indispensable Qualities of A Leader by John C. Maxwell. (1999, Thomas Nelson)

Who Moved My Cheese? by Spencer Johnson. (1998, G. P. Putnam & Sons)

The Seat of the Soul by Gary Zukav. (1989, Simon & Schuster)

The Millionaire Mind by Spencer Johnson. (2000, Andrew McMeel)

On Becoming a Leader by Warren Bennis. (1989, Addison-Wesley)

If Success Is a Game These Are the Rules by Cherie Carter-Scott, Ph.D. (2000, Broadway Books)

Think Like a Champion by Mike Shanahan. (1999, Harper Business)

The Model Leader by William Hitt. (1993, Battelle Press)

Simple Steps to Impossible Dreams by Steven K. Scott (1998, Simon & Schuster)

LUCENT'S WINNING CFO TEAM

The following article, "Transforming Lucent's CFO," by Thomas A. Francesconi, is reproduced, with permission, from the July 1998 issue of *Management Accounting*. The magazine is published by the Institute of Management Accountants in Montvale, New Jersey. All text and graphics included are copyright © by the Institute of Management Accountants unless otherwise noted.

Transforming L

BY THOMAS A. FRANCESCONI

Four years ago, Lucent Technologies' CFO operation needed an overhaul. A benchmarking study revealed that its transaction-processing side was costly and inefficient, and it came up short in the "best practices" area. What could it do to improve? The company took a hard look at itself, then instituted an elaborate plan to create a cultural paradigm shift. Today the CFO organization is well on its way to transforming itself from a cost center into a competitive, world-class business. Here's the secret to its success.

BENCHMARKING CFO

Lucent Technologies, formerly known as Western Electric and then AT&T Network Systems, became a stand-alone company on October 1, 1996, when AT&T separated into three companies. (The other two are the new AT&T and NCR.) Lucent, supported by Bell Laboratories, designs, develops, manufactures, and markets communications systems and technologies ranging from microchips to whole networks.

Throughout 1994 and 1995, Lucent's CFO operation, while still embedded in various divisions and subsidiaries of AT&T, became involved in a benchmarking initiative that compared its costs with those of "best-in-class" companies. Company representatives worked with an outside consultant who manages a database containing current data on financial processes for more than 1,100 companies. They compared Lucent's financial processes to those of 22 other large companies in various industries with revenues ranging from $5 billion to $90 billion and with financial staffs of up to 15,000 employees.

The benchmarking data revealed that the cost of Lucent's CFO organization was significantly greater than that of several best-in-class companies. Inefficiencies fell primarily into the areas of staffing and systems (related costs included salaries, benefits, overtime, outside services such as for temps and contractors, system development, processing, storage, and

Everyone is working toward the goal of costing the corporation no more than 1% of revenue.

printing). Benchmarking also revealed that the most efficient CFO organizations were operating at or below 1% of revenue. Lucent would have to make some significant changes to its systems and processes before it could operate that efficiently.

A NEW COMPANY

Lucent's change initiative began in early 1996 when it started the process toward becoming stand-alone. At that time, the CFO organization's mission was clear: Revamp systems and

Accounts payable colleagues in Alpharetta, Ga., exhibit the spirit behind Lucent's Team CFO initiative.

processes to meet its goal of costing the corporation no more than 1% of revenue, one of the benchmarks associated with the existing best-in-class companies.

An important step was to design a mission statement and develop a program that would let the workforce know exactly what was going on and what would be expected of them. Under the leadership of Don Peterson, executive vice president and chief financial officer, and Jim Lusk, controller, the concept of Team CFO was developed. The goal was to have the

ucent's CFO

CFO organization be a key strategic partner in the formulation and implementation of Lucent strategies. It would furnish Lucent with finance functions that would allow its internal business partners to provide more competitive services to their customers. Then the people in the CFO organization would be seen as positive contributors to corporate results. The group adopted a souped-up race car as its symbol (Team CFO...Engine of Excellence...Powering Lucent) and began "racing to the future together." (See sidebar on "Reinventing CFO," p. 28.)

Don Peterson and his leadership team, composed of representatives from the various branches of the CFO organization, established four "Conditions of Satisfaction" to make their intentions clear to all CFO colleagues. (Lucent employees are now called colleagues to reflect the new corporate culture that emphasizes everyone working together as respectful business partners.) They are:

- 100% of our business partners acknowledge Team CFO as strategic partners in achieving Lucent objectives by 12/31/98.
- 100% of Team CFO agrees that we live our values and purpose.
- Total CFO budget is less than or equal to 1% of Lucent revenue by calendar year 1998.
- Financial modules of SAP implemented Lucent-wide by 12/31/98.

These Conditions of Satisfaction continue to reflect specific milestones in the CFO organization's journey toward becoming a world-class business.

To accomplish these goals, Lucent's diverse and globally scattered CFO organization would have to work as a team, capitalizing on the ability to share systems and expertise among departments. The operation consists of three main branches: Policy, SME (subject matter experts), and Corporate Center Support; Business Analysis and Decision Support (finance people reporting within the various business units); and Business Support for Transactions (also known as Lucent Financial Services). (See the Shared Services Model illustration. The majority of this article is about the "financial processing" organization within LFS—Danny Lanier's organization. Danny reports to Controller Jim Lusk, who reports to CFO Don Peterson.)

Implementation of SAP, the German-based enterprisewide financial system, would satisfy at least two urgent needs of the business. It would reduce manual intervention within financial processes and allow the financial systems to accommodate dates beyond 1999.

SHARED SERVICES MODEL: TEAM CFO

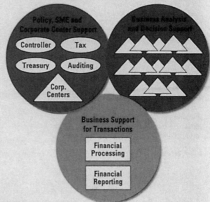

A QUANTUM LEAP

Significant changes took place within our branch of the CFO organization, Business Support for Transactions. Most of Lucent CFO's transaction-intensive operations are located in Alpharetta, Ga., where more than 800 Lucent colleagues perform various accounting, inventory, invoicing, accounts receivable, collections, analysis, payroll, and accounts payable functions for the corporation. (Lucent has about 130,000 colleagues overall.) Danny Lanier, director of Lucent Financial Services' Financial Process (LFS Financial Process) in Alpharetta, met the challenge of reducing costs and becoming more efficient head-on. In March 1996, he called a meeting with his Financial Services leadership team to devise a plan that would accomplish two seemingly contradictory objectives: (1) lower costs, and (2) improve service to internal customers—so much that the term *strategic business partner* would describe the new relationship.

The leadership team immediately got to work on brainstorming, process by process, how they would transform LFS Financial Process into a state-of-the-art, world-class operation. Each process owner was charged with:

- Identifying their competitors (mainly firms offering to perform financial functions via outsourcing arrangements) and learning their strategy.

■ Performing primary research through professional organizations, consulting firms, publications, and benchmarking efforts to identify industry best practices for each financial function Lucent's CFO organization performed.

■ Developing a list of specific projects with estimated costs, benefits, and implementation intervals that would drive down costs to meet or exceed industry benchmarks within a three-year time frame.

Later that month, Danny Lanier sent a memorandum to all colleagues, telling them about the plan, soliciting their help to make the identified projects a success, and asking for suggestions. We dubbed the three-year plan Project Quantum Leap (PQL) because of the aggressive schedule we proposed to reduce costs and improve processes.

BEST PRACTICES WE IDENTIFIED (OR INVENTED)

We identified several key projects to drive costs down and service levels up. Most of these "best practices," described below, are in various stages of implementation.

Accounts payable: *We are striving for "paperless" payables.* Approximately 60% of the invoices processed by Lucent's accounts payable group are paid electronically, and the percentage is increasing. In its quest for a paperless operation, accounts payable has several initiatives under way:

■ Implementation of a procurement card for noninventory purchases under $1,000 (excluding travel and living). The goal of the "PRO Card" program is to reduce the volume of paper invoices and accompanying manual processes. In its fully deployed state, procurement card transactions are expected to account for 30% of the manual invoice volume. Over 15% of the volume already has been eliminated through use of the procurement card.

■ Mandatory use of electronic vouchering for travel and living expenses. More than 80% of the workforce was using the existing electronic vouchering program, but only 4% were using e-mail for voucher submission and approval. The majority of employees were printing out their vouchers and using the hard-copy process of securing approval. This procedure required several people to handle paper, and someone had to input the information manually into the accounts payable system from the paper voucher. With e-mail, the process is now direct from colleague to computer.

■ More widespread use of electronic data interchange (EDI) for doing business with suppliers and an "evaluated receipts settlement" (ERS) system, which pays for factory supplies electronically upon receipt. At the inception of the project, only 30% to 35% of business was handled through a combination of EDI and ERS, and use of ERS was only 1%. Today, approximately 45% of invoices are processed through EDI and ERS.

■ Perhaps the most pressing demand on any accounts payable operation is reporting the status of invoice payments. Thousands of requests for status on any given invoice come in each month from suppliers, procurement managers, factories, and employees. Best-in-class companies inevitably find efficient ways of dealing with inquiries.

LFS Financial Process is reducing the use of labor-intense customer "hotlines" and is offering its customers alternatives such as online or recorded-voice access to the status of any given invoice.

Payroll. *We are consolidating our payroll systems under SAP.* Lucent's payroll system actually had evolved into five separate systems because of differing needs among business units. We created a manual system to handle special "between cycles" payments such as for special awards or for producing checks for new employees who were hired between payroll processing cycles. Separate line operations groups were needed to accommodate the idiosyncrasies of each system. Accounting became complicated and redundant. Multiple accounts were set up to accommodate the five payroll processes. These disadvantages will be addressed when the payroll systems are combined. The first of the five payroll systems, supporting approximately 13,000 colleagues, is scheduled to be converted to SAP in October 1998. The other four are expected to be converted by the end of 1999.

Doug Krey, l., director of payroll services, and Terry Easley, director-billing, accounts receivable, Treasury Operations, enjoy a recent open communications session (see p. 30).

We are simplifying payroll practices. A review of the payroll process made it clear that we needed organized guidelines on how to handle special requests, deductions, interim payments, and loans. In the past, the corporate culture dictated almost never saying "no" to any special payroll request. For example, a payroll line group would work all weekend meeting a deadline to have a batch of special award checks printed for one of the business units. Now such practices are rare. Alternatives, such as including award money in employees' regular paychecks, are more common.

Recently, a new process was implemented to handle payroll underpayments. (Underpayments generally result from late time reporting, allotments deducted in error, and late benefit approval.) To avoid issuing manual interim paychecks, along

STRIVING FOR PAPERLESS PAYABLES A SUCCESS STORY

"Paperless" payables comprise about 60% of Lucent's transactions. Leading the charge toward a paperless environment are:

Procurement Card

Lucent has issued more than 24,000 procurement cards to employees who initiate approximately 60,000 transactions per month, making it MasterCard's number one procurement card customer. Prime targets for the "Pro Card" are small purchases for items such as office supplies, periodicals, subscriptions, express mail, maintenance and repair, software, and fax machines. The cost (per transaction) of approving and paying a monthly credit card bill is only about 5% of the cost of approving and processing traditional purchase requisitions. Implementation of the Pro Card has had a significant impact on the ability of the accounts payable organization to shrink amidst the increased volumes of transactions resulting from Lucent's growth and acquisitions over the last two years.

Accounts payable pays $4 million+ invoices per year. When handled manually, a host of activities must take place that are not necessary via the PRO Card. For manual invoices you must:

- first create a purchase order;
- open mail upon receipt of an invoice;
- have data entry enter an invoice into the system;
- create a vendor record in system (if not already there);
- handle inquiries, investigations, corrections;
- produce and mail a check.

The average time to pay could be as high as 45 days. With the Pro Card, processing payments for small items is much easier. Like any credit card, it is a matter of paying a monthly invoice for all purchases to the bank. Vendors receive their payments from the bank in an average of three days versus 45 days.

Electronic Data Interchange (EDI)

Initiating purchases of large-ticket items, such as inventory, is best handled electronically. EDI functions include the electronic placement of purchase orders with vendors and electronic invoicing from vendors to accounts payable. The EDI process benefits accounts payable because it eliminates a manual invoice being rendered by a vendor. It also provides for an automatic match between the purchase order and the invoice as business is conducted computer-to-computer. Lucent has experienced a 15% increase in EDI transactions over the past year and continues to woo vendors over to electronic commerce.

Evaluated Receipts Settlement (ERS)

This is a variation of the EDI process that eliminates the need to wait for an invoice. Payment for goods received is triggered by the receiving process, usually at the dock. When goods are received at a factory dock, they are entered into a receiving system that simultaneously triggers payment. The vendor does not render an invoice; therefore, the accounts payable organization does not have an invoice to enter into any system. The vendor tracks payment by using the packing slip number.

with calculating deductions and taxes, new guidelines were issued that provide for (1) waiting until the next pay cycle for the correction or (2) issuing an advance—a much simpler procedure—in cases where the dollars involved are significant.

Many wage deductions either have been or are being considered for elimination, including employee wage loans, the ability to have purchases deducted from employees' paychecks, commercial life insurance deductions, political action committee deductions, and deductions for safety shoes and glasses.

We are increasing the use of electronic funds transfer (EFT). Increasing the use of "paperless" checks greatly reduces manual intervention. Now approximately 80% of paychecks are issued via EFT. The final 20% represent a "tremendous challenge" according to Doug Krey, financial director of the payroll team. These colleagues are determined to cash their checks personally, and they reject the idea of EFT. Lucent has not yet decided to make EFT mandatory. Several alternatives are being reviewed.

Accounts receivable. *We are mechanizing subledger reconciliation as much as possible via SAP.* This process primarily involves synchronizing postings to the general ledger and subledger, which is a manual process in the older legacy mainframe systems.

We are increasing the speed of lining up payments with the appropriate invoices for customers with multiple purchases. Remittance information accompanying international wire payments, for example, sometimes is incomplete. We have increased partnering with customers, banks, and Lucent field representatives to make sure that all payments are accompanied by detailed remittance information. Benchmarking with several companies turned up some novel approaches to the cash application problem such as allowing customers to apply their own payment via dial-up or Internet programs. We are exploring these new approaches to see if they are compatible with Lucent's processes. Internet invoicing is now available for some customers. The cash applications feature will be the next step. Internal benchmarking with Lucent's accounts payable and treasury organizations is shedding light on what issues and challenges payers have in attempting to pay multiple invoices via EDI, mail, and wire transfer.

Treasury operations. Lucent's Treasury Operations organization is in the process of implementing a software package to identify check fraud and encoding errors online before a check clears, thereby reducing manual intervention as well as misappropriated funds.

Inventory. *We are striving for greater accuracy and speed in inventory accounting.* System improvements have been put in place to improve the process of matching the cost of billable products and services among inventory, sales, and downstream accounting systems. Tracking inventory at a less detailed level has helped speed up the reconciliation process while maintaining reporting integrity.

Measurements. *We have increased emphasis on internal measurements.* The team created measurements or "vital signs" for key functions. Measurements are either customer focused—used to measure performance in terms of customer expectations—or efficiency focused—used to measure internal efficiencies and costs. Examples of customer-focused measurements are response time or ratings from customer satisfaction surveys. Efficiency measurements are used mostly for comparing or "benchmarking" processes with those of best-in-class firms. Examples are cycle time, rate of defects, and cost per transaction.

Understanding costs. Tools and techniques for understanding costs and causes of costs, such as activity-based costing (ABC) systems, are common in manufacturing organizations. Modified versions of ABC also can be used in service organizations in cost reduction programs and for allocating costs equitably among business units. LFS Financial Process has employed ABC concepts in setting up a tracking system for these purposes. We set up cost "pools" by financial process. We identified cost drivers, such as the number of payroll payments, accounts payable payments, and accounting transactions. We included a process for tracking direct labor by business unit. One benefit of the ABC approach was that it let us perform root cause analyses in areas identified as having a high potential for cost savings.

THE TOUGH PART

Our experience with Project Quantum Leap so far is that some projects proceed according to plan, while others run into difficulty—either organizational or logistical. (See sidebars on pp. 26, 27.) The keys to success, however, are the commitments made by the team leaders to operate under substantially reduced budgets. Therefore, when one project fails, another is put in its place. Although projects sometimes are changed or replaced, financial commitments remain the same.

An additional challenge pertains to the timing of Lucent's decision to outsource a significant portion of its computer programming and development work to a subsidiary of IBM. The success of many Project Quantum Leap activities is dependent upon mechanizing manual processes. Therefore, a successful transition of development work from LFS Financial Process colleagues to IBM has been, and still is, critical. Furthermore, choices between implementing improvements in existing systems versus waiting for an SAP solution arise constantly as the SAP implementation schedule for each of the financial processes evolves.

THE STATUS OF PROJECT QUANTUM LEAP

It appears that LFS will make its commitment to reduce costs while implementing process improvements within the planned time frames. We surpassed our 1996 and 1997 targets, and we are operating within our reduced 1998 budget because of the collective benefit of many process improvements. Implementation of SAP is taking place slower than expected because of the complexities built into the older legacy systems, but the corporation remains committed to working out the kinks. General ledger and payroll modules are still scheduled for implementation before the end of 1998. For accounts payable, SAP has been implemented for one of our business units—BCS (Business Communications Systems) already. We are processing about $1 million per day in invoic-

LESSON LEARNED— WHAT DIDN'T WORK

Historically, the accounts payable organization handled external and internal customer inquires personally, via telephone "hotlines." Vendors would call for assistance when reconciling their accounts receivable balances. Internal business unit and procurement department customers would call to investigate the status of individual invoices. In essence, customers would count on getting personal attention from an accessible accounts payable colleague when they called.

In the early stages of Project Quantum Leap, the accounts payable hotlines were discontinued. The rationale was that the colleagues answering telephones could be put to better use paying and investigating invoices. (The thinking was that inquiries would diminish as more resources were used to pay invoices in record time.) Customers were notified of the change in the process, and a telephone contact list was issued for cases where personal assistance was still needed.

Customers immediately let the accounts payable management team know how they felt about the discontinuance of the hotlines. They said they had lost the personal service to which they were accustomed and that it had become too difficult to reach a live colleague. In frustration, they began calling the accounts payable managers for help, which, of course, tied up the management team, making it difficult for them to perform their responsibilities. What had started out as a process improvement was quickly becoming a process nightmare.

The accounts payable leadership team responded to the customers' outcry quickly and decisively. Hotlines were put back in place in combination with a voice response system. Now routine inquiries are handled 24 hours a day using the automated line, which has reduced the volume of calls to the hotlines. Vendors continue to praise the decision to implement the voice response system because it has become a useful tool for reconciling their accounts receivable balances, allowing them to verify the status of outstanding invoices any time they choose.

In retrospect, the accounts payable leadership team realized that they originally underestimated their customers' perceived need for personal service. Customers had become used to personal contact and interpreted the loss of it as a negative. Change had to come gradually because an entrenched corporate culture existed.

The combined system of automated voice response and personal contact has turned a volatile situation into a win-win proposition for customers and suppliers. Internet solutions as well the implementation of SAP will enhance the process further—as a world-class accounts payable process evolves.

REINVENTING CFO

CFO Don Peterson is committed to his organization being a strategic business partner within Lucent Technologies. The concept of Team CFO...Engine of Excellence...Powering Lucent represents that commitment. According to Don, CFO is not content with merely reporting the financial state of the business; we are focused on participating in the planning and executing of the corporate vision, i.e., driving and steering the business, looking forward. According to our strategic intent training, we are to "stand in the future," look back at where we are—and get to where we need to be.

We define a strategic business partner as being: one who (1) knows the fundamentals of Lucent's businesses, including the basis by which Lucent competes in the market and how the business itself creates value for customers; (2) knows Lucent's products and those of its competitors; (3) is a change leader in strategic cost management techniques that are applicable to the business.

According to Jim Lusk, Lucent's controller, "...this is about being a business, about being on time, at cost, with quality and ahead of competition. It's not just being process focused, but focused on solving business problems. This thinking is about having a clear line of sight to our external customers and questioning our every action to be certain of the value we provide."

The cultural changes taking place within Lucent Financial Services can be summed up in the following statement, which is displayed prominently throughout the organization:

"Incredibly Awesome Partner Service... Delivered By Incredibly Awesome People"

Bringing about cultural change takes more than presenting information via posters, fliers, and speeches. To help CFO colleagues personalize the new way of doing business and interacting with each other, "strategic intent" coaching sessions were offered. Facilitated through the assistance of an external change management firm, the training encouraged colleagues to communicate effectively, make clear requests of each other with appropriate time frames, declare breakdowns where necessary, and to strive for breakthroughs in thinking and processes. The three-day training program consisted of a combination of lectures, role playing exercises, team projects and fun. The CFO "Ignition Team" coordinated the training and encouraged full participation from all our global colleagues.

Today, it is apparent that we are results-focused, team-based business partners. Communication is open and honest. Preconceived ideas, termed as one's "already thinking," via the strategic intent training, are put aside, allowing for creativity, focus, and speed. We communicate not only content but context when dealing with each other—which further enhances our understanding of goals and intent.

es for BCS in SAP. Other business units are scheduled for implementation in October, December, and out to the year 2002. BCS also is using SAP already for order entry and material management.

The remaining challenges are to reduce colleagues' stress in the wake of the rapid change that has taken place and to gain business partners' confidence that service will not deteriorate but will actually improve over the next few years. Lucent is using information-gathering tools such as surveys, communications sessions, and customer conferences to keep the doors of communication open among LFS, its colleagues, and its business partners.

A 1998 survey of LFS Financial Process colleagues showed that, overall, their views on organizational leadership have improved since a similar 1996 survey. Evaluating their supervisors, colleagues gave high scores in the following areas:

- "Gives me authority to do my job and serve customers."
- "Demonstrates obsession with serving customers."
- "Demonstrates personal accountability."
- "Has my respect."

Areas where opportunities for improvement still exist include:

- "Has created an environment where it is safe to say what you think and/or challenge traditional methods."
- "Builds teamwork, not competition."
- "Effectively deals with change [and] uncertainty."

A December 1997 survey of the internal customers of CFO disclosed that 75% agreed that CFO is considered a strategic partner in achieving Lucent objectives—up from 55% in January of 1997. Goals are to improve these results to 100% by the end of 1998.

WHAT TEAM MEMBERS THINK

The surveys were informative, but we also wanted to hear directly from some Team CFO members. I walked the hallways and stopped people at random to get their views on the changes that have been taking place. I talked with management and nonmanagement and made sure I got a good cross section of the processes (accounts payable, payroll, accounts receivable, inventory). Here is what I heard:

"If we are going to be a powerful company, we need to move forward with implementation of SAP. I would like to see our CFO take a stronger stance with the business units and require quicker implementation."

"I like the idea of not just being an expense to the corporation. I like being a strategic partner." "Some folks still have the old mindset...keep to yourself, don't let anyone know what you really do...for fear that they will take your job. It's time we all work together as a team."

"I'm doing pretty well. Most of us are adjusting. It's nice to see people getting promoted—not that I've been offered one yet." "It was good to see that a five-year contract was negotiated [with the union] recently. It shows that the company is serious, and that it values its colleagues."

"I think we are moving in the right direction with all of the training. It helps you understand where other people

OPEN COMMUNICATIONS

Danny Lanier, director of Lucent Financial Services' Financial Process, is committed to the concept of full disclosure, or communicating openly and honestly with LFS colleagues both in good and not-so-good times. One of the methods he uses to keep folks informed is what has become known as Open Communications Sessions, held at least once a month.

He uses this time to update everyone on what's happening with the business and with the reorganization of CFO, and he shares any other information he considers pertinent. In these meetings, Danny consistently acknowledges and supports the "Workplace of the Future" program; a partnership between management and the Communication Workers of America, where CWA members actively participate in decisions affecting their jobs. He encourages discussion and questions pertaining to all aspects of work at LFS.

In one recent session, Danny shared his personal performance appraisal with everyone. He acknowledged his gaps and explained that it's okay to have gaps as long as you know what they are and that you are committed to working on them. Through the acknowledgment of gaps you can improve the way that you perform.

Often at Open Communication Sessions individuals are given recognition for a job well done. Last year, monetary awards were given to individuals who had suggested money-saving process improvements that had been implemented.

The Open Communications Sessions have been a huge success. Division and district managers have followed suit, and have implemented similar sessions for their specific work groups.

Danny Lanier

are coming from. My job is pretty much the same. I would like to see change occur faster."

"In our position, answering inquiries, handling complaints, overall troubleshooting, it's hard to think of ourselves as business partners. We still think of ourselves as customer service ... maybe if we were promoted to being a developer or something ... where we interacted more from a planning standpoint."

Despite these mixed reviews, colleagues are still committed to overall success.

THE NEW CFO MODEL

Lucent Technologies' CFO has almost completed its reorganization under a shared-services model where similar or redundant functions performed within individual business units and the corporate controller's organization are being combined. Many financial functions previously performed within the business units have been transferred to LFS, and LFS financial "hubs" have been established internationally. These hubs are located in Mexico, Argentina, Brazil, Singapore, China, Ireland, and the Netherlands.

Prior to the shared services organization, you could find virtually everything we do replicated within Lucent's business units. Although not all finance functions have been physically relocated (what some refer to as the "brick and mortar approach"), they are being managed and coordinated centrally. We have gained many efficiencies and synergies via this shared services concept.

LFS Financial Process, under the leadership of Danny Lanier, is the largest hub for financial services in the new environment. Our 1998 operating costs are running about 40% less than they were at the inception of Project Quantum Leap, service levels have improved, and stress levels are declining.

Now we truly see ourselves as strategic business partners within Lucent. We realize our systems and processes can affect the quality and speed of delivering Lucent's products and services, and we are working hard to make sure we are meeting everyone's targets. When asked what key ingredients have made Project Quantum Leap successful, Danny Lanier commented, "The commitment and sacrifices made by all LFS colleagues, top-down measurable commitments, a willingness to learn from others, and the project-by-project approach to continuous process improvement." ■

Thomas A. Francesconi, CIA, CQM, is financial planning and quality manager at Lucent Technologies Inc. in Alpharetta, Ga. He can be reached at (770) 750-4272, phone, or e-mail, francesconi@lucent.com.

Danny Lanier, Founder and President
MaxpoCoach
P.O. Box 213
Alpharetta, GA 30009

Office: 770-667-8346   Fax: 770-667-1804
E-Mail: 4dlanier@bellsouth.net

Dear Reader:

Someone asked me how I came up with the title of this book: *Setting the Pace for Business Success.* I explained that after I'd been taking notes of my impressions and insights for about ten years, I had a drawer full of information, and I said, "This is too much." So wherever I had duplication, I threw out the extras. I kept reducing the collection until I got it down to four things that I identified as business success factors: performance, attitude, character, and exposure. Take the first letters of those words (P-A-C-E) and see how I made use of them in the title.

I continued to work at this over the years and, as I got closer to retirement, I discovered some new things I thought needed to be highlighted. Of course, what I identified grew beyond performance, attitude, character, and exposure, as you can tell when you read the book or examine the table of contents.

Borrowing from that experience, it was easy to name my new venture. I coach others to maximize their potential. So the name *MaxpoCoach* is a natural. Although I began to plan for it five years earlier, MaxpoCoach was officially born in January 2001.

In the last 60 to 90 days, I've presented seminars on leadership and personal development. Those will continue as I provide one-on-one coaching services based primarily on the contents of this book but also based upon experiences that may not be included in the book.

I'll be coaching via the telephone!

My fee can be lower because travel time and travel expenses are eliminated. Coaching can take place at almost any time during reasonable hours. So far, the people I coach initiated the calls because I haven't done any advertising. We plan a mutually agreeable time to talk and we keep the appointment.

I invite you to contact me to:
- Discuss how a coach may be of specific service to you. It can be MaxpoCoach or another coach.
- Talk about any of the topics discussed in this book.
- Ask for advice or share insights you have that relate to *Setting the Pace for Business Success*.

Pick the contact method you prefer. Information on how to reach me appears at the top of this letter. I'll get back to you within 72 hours of receipt of your request. Be aware that I may not receive your request quickly when I'm out of town to present a seminar.

Over the years, I've told co-workers that people remember most things that get done that others thought couldn't be done. Just because someone says you can't put a bowling ball through a garden hose, it just means that nobody has done it yet.

If you need a little support to make something wonderful happen for you, contact me! Don't delay. I look forward to hearing from you.

Sincerely,

Danny Lanier

Danny Lanier

INDEX